WAR *from a* CHILD'S POINT OF VIEW

ELIZABETH UKENI ABAMU

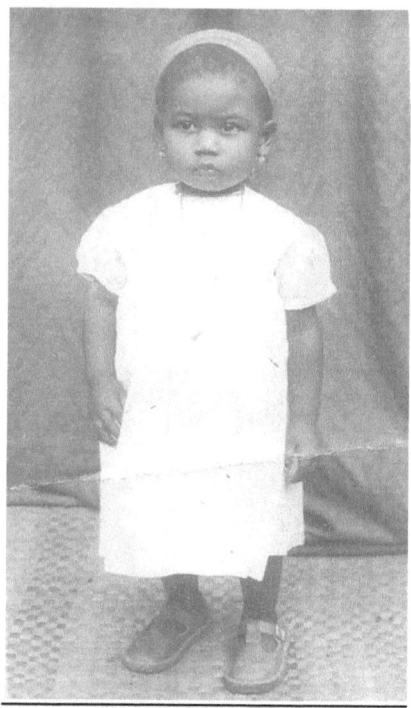

One Year Young Elizabeth:

*My adopted attitude was that I had a spot light
shining on me and when it periodically went out
the halo over my head would become visible.
I had confidence without knowing it, an inviting
temperament without feeling it, and a hopeful future
that I always knew did not depend on me alone.*

Contact: Email: warfromachildspointofview@yahoo.com
Website/Blog: warfromachildspointofview.wordpress.com
Like us on Face Book "War from a Child's Point of View"

First Edition
Second Print

Cover Designer & Mentor: Dr. Anthony Obi Ogbo
Editors: Alan Jacobson
        Jenny U. Abamu Akbas
        Dr. Ejim Nkama Sule
Additional Editing: Don Okolo

SPECIAL THANKS & APPECIATION
To all who supported, assisted, and encouraged me in various ways to
complete and publish this book: Kate Ofodile, Dr. Emeaba Emeaba,
Rev. Aluu W. Nnali, Bridgette Deborah Bennett, Ngozi Ikweke, Rose
Abamu, Mary Ukeni, Nicky Abamu, Sirisha Hasan, Ngozi Obiaku,
Sally Ikemba, Sheila Snow, B.J. Perez, Kingsley & Vicky Oka, Bishop
Ethel George, Bishop T. D. Jakes who pastors my soul, Joel
Osteenwho encourages my soul, Dr. David Jeremiah & Chuck
Swindoll who minister to my soul.

Contents .... Pages

Dedication 5
Forward 6

CHAPTERS

1. The First Bomb 15
2. Family 23
3. The Journey Home 27
4. Life in Our Hometown 34
5. The farms 39
6. The New Yam Festivals 67
7. The Exodus 76
8. Home Away From Home 82
9. Another Exodus 100
10. A surprise Visitor 121
11. The War Ends 140
12. A Different Kind of War Starts 147
13. The return Home 159
14. The Aftermath of War 176
15. Back to the Farms 196
16. Rebuilding Unwana 216
17. My Last Days in Unwana 223
18. That was then and this is now......... 252
    About the Author 276
    REFERENCES & PICTURES SOURCES 279

DEDICATION

This book is dedicated to my children: Alex, Jenny, Zabeth, and Andrew; to my mother Gloria, and my late grandmother, Mma Jenny.

I thank my children for their positive influence, encouragement, and push to complete this book, my mother for always loving, providing, encouraging, and being available for us all, and then my grandmother for all her exemplary teachings that has positioned me to always strive for the best with a spirit of excellence.

I give God all the glory for our lives and all the abilities He has given us to make positive contributions to society in this time that we live in.

FOREWARD

Many a times when men have declared wars, they could have compromised for peaceful resolutions like that of the Billy Goats in the middle of a narrow bridge. My grandmother, Mma Jenny, first told me this old story when we returned to our demolished hometown after three years of an unjust Nigerian and Biafran civil war.

A Billy Goat was on its way to the green pastures where other animals also came to graze. There was a narrow bridge they all had to cross when going to or leaving the pasture field. The bridge was so narrow that only one animal could pass it at a time. One day, as one Billy Goat was leaving the pastures, another was going to it and they both met at the middle of this narrow bridge. They argued a bit as to what to do, as one said to the other, "you go back and let me cross first," and the other said the same. Out of frustration one suggested that they should fight it out and after which the survival of the fittest would cross. The other Billy Goat then said, "I have a better suggestion". "Ok, said the other "let's hear it." The wise Billy Goat then suggested, "Why not allow one of us to lie down on the ground while the other walks over? Neither one of us will have to go back; neither will anyone get hurt, nor waste any more precious time." The other Billy Goat got wisdom from that council and agreed. So, one Billy Goat lay down while the other walked over him and they both went on their way as winners.

My grandmother pointed out to me that the Billy Goats did not let their ego get in the way as to who would be the one to walk over the other, as long as the end result was fruitful and a win-win for both. They both agreed and executed a peaceful resolution and no one ever had to know who lay down for the other to cross over. In the sight of some men, the one who stooped down would be considered weak and maybe stupid, but in the sight of God and other wise men and women, he would be considered humble, meek, and peaceable.

Many past wars could have been prevented and future wars can still be prevented by providing and accepting peaceful resolutions by our leaders. Nothing is won by force. Momentarily, it may seem to the victors as they brag about their conquest and gather up the spoils, that they have victory. With time, the seeds of bloodshed of the innocent blossom into harvests of deranged populations of unruly avengers that become an undesired part of the spoils and the world population.

Rebuilding structures after a ravaged war is the easy part; the hardest part is renewing the minds of the masses victimized by any war. The shed blood of the innocent, the curses hurled from the mouths of the victims of war onto the initiators of unjust wars, I believe sticks on them. They never really have the peace to live in the luxury of the so called peaceful zones of their domains. The wars within them consume them. "He who lives by the sword shall die by the sword" is a judgment that becomes of the sword bearer, whether one bears the sword by him or herself, or bears it through the hands of another.

The cause of the Nigerian and Biafran civil war was a combination of political, economic, ethnic, cultural, and religious tension between the dominating Nigerian Northerners and the Southerners who became intolerant to the built up oppression. After Britain decolonized the region, tensions between tribes in the north and south were forced to face off in the new Nigeria. The economic stress was birthed out of the Northerners' control and distribution of the crude oil production which lies underneath the soil in the Southeastern Region of Nigeria. Southerners viewed the resource as part of their land and felt that the Northerners exploited their resources unjustly.

The Northern Region is mostly dry desert land. The Northerners wanted the crude oil refineries to be placed in their region and the crude oil siphoned to their region through miles of pipe lines they proposed to lay across the country.

The Southeasterners refused and chose to separate from Nigeria. They formed a new country called Biafra led by Odumegwu Ojukwu. The Northerners rejected the separation as they would no longer have crude oil as a natural resource; a major revenue the whole country enjoyed and depended on, which was and still is the major international market resource. Each side took an 'all or nothing' approach and war became inevitable. The 'first punch' was thrown by the Northerners led by Yakubu Gowon. "One Nigeria" became a vocal slogan that was not practiced in the hearts of our leaders or most indigenes even till this day, thus the satisfaction of a harmonious resolution was far reached.

In countries like Nigeria, politics and religion are mixed up like water and oil, and there are constant attempts to shake them profusely to get them to stay mixed, but whenever the shaking stops, the two will naturally separate again with religion always on top. Northerners, who are predominantly Muslims, disliked the Southeasterners who are predominantly Christian, and vice versa. The Northerners killed a lot of the Christians who lived among them, and those who escaped returned to the East with gruesome pictures and documented stories of the atrocities and genocides afflicted on a people.

Pregnant Ibo women had their babies cut out of their wombs and the corpses of their fetus laid on top of the bellies of their mothers' dead bodies. Many had their eyes gorged out or blinded with hot iron placed close to their eyes and scorched. Many Ibos were butchered and their body parts laid on un-tarred dusty roads of Northern Nigeria leading to the train stations as they tried to escape. There were so many recorded and unrecorded atrocities and horror stories that were relayed to the adults as we, the children, overheard by eavesdropping into their conversation. Sometimes they were so engrossed talking and listening to each other that they forgot we, the children, were in their mist.

In retaliation, the Northerners who lived in the East were sent packing to go back to their region of the country. Biafra was birthed and her leaders installed, after which the three year Nigerian and Biafran war started in 1967. With the help of special interests, Nigeria won and the Biafran name was buried in defeat and shame, but also in relief. As Commander in Chief, Odumegwu Ojukwu, self-exiled to Ivory Coast, the crude oil which was mostly the spoil, was then controlled by the Northerners, and so has it been to this day.

I have pondered these words from the mouth of my grandmother in my heart over the years. I have grown to now appreciate her and consider her as a very wise woman. I prayed to have wisdom like she did or be wiser than she was, in order to positively impact others and people that are led into my life and sphere of influence during and after my time. I believe God has blessed me with knowledge, understanding, and wisdom to write this civil war story, that I believe could have been avoided if our leaders pressed for a peaceful resolution like the Billy Goats did.

The viewpoints in this book are all from a child's point of view, from observations, thoughts, and the things I heard as a child growing up during that war era. Much has changed since then, some for the worst and some for the best. My grandmother has since gone home to be with the Lord at a good old age of over 90 years, but her legacy lives on as a transferred chunk of knowledge, understanding, and wisdom from her to me and to you the blessed reader.

CHAPTER 1

The First Bomb

It was either late August or early September of 1967 that I remembered over hearing my parents speaking in low but panicky voices. They did not seem to be fighting or quarreling. My father, very sober this time, told my mother that he was going out to some other barrister's house to see if he could get some more current information about a potential war. My mother stayed home to attend to my twin baby sister and brother who were a little over a month old. I was eleven years young myself and had a lot of responsibilities in helping out with caring for my new born twins siblings. I asked my mother what the matter was and she said that I did not need to worry, and that all will be fine, so I did not.

My father returned about two hours later and was stopped by one of our neighbors and his wife who raised her voice in a cry of desperation as my father told them whatever it was that was going on. Mother heard my father's voice and hurried out with the baby boy in her arms to join the heated conversation. As I followed her at a comfortable distance, all I could hear was that rebels were heading to this town that we lived in, called Abakaliki, so we had to find a way out since the Biafran Armed Forces had security check points and barricades at various places on the road, and were not letting anyone leave.

I started to become very concerned and worried. The same ill feeling of despair that I always felt when my father came home from work in the evenings drunk returned. It was an uptight, sick feeling that made my stomach ache, a feeling of desperate fear and uncertainty. Truly, fear of losing my mother to the violence that followed whenever he returned home from work drunk. I also felt that she would fear for her life and run away, or be killed in the domestic violence. This ill feeling kept me wide awake most nights wondering if things would ever be alright.

The next morning I realized that I had fallen asleep after all. My father had left for work and my mother was feeding my baby brother. I asked to help, she said that I can take the already made baby food and feed his twin sister.

My baby brother was born with his umbilical cord around his neck and the muscle strength around his neck was weak, therefore he had to be held very carefully. We nicknamed him 'rubber neck'. Only adults were allowed to pick him up at the time. As my mother was explaining to me the circumstances surrounding his birth, we heard an extremely loud passenger plane. We all ran outside and saw the huge aircraft flying so low that it seemed like we could almost touch it. It flew slow and over our heads. It hovered

Just a few minutes later we heard a loud BANG!
An earthquake like vibration seemed
to shake the whole world.

around the market area. Then we lost sight of it. Just a few minutes later we heard the loudest BANG! An 'earthquake like' vibration seemed to shake the whole world. With great panic everybody in the house and in the yard where we lived ran in every direction looking for shelter and or a place to hide from the loud bang no one had any understanding of. There was total chaos. No one was prepared or educated to handle this sudden impact, nor was any one self-controlled enough to calm others. The passenger plane then moved up higher and left the air space.

After a few hours people ran into the yard to report that the loud noise was from a huge bomb thrown from that passenger plane into the market place and this had formed one of the largest holes ever seen. "People were in panic, abandoned their goods and ran for their lives" stated a young lady who had witnessed the market bombing. The next day the market place was deserted, and also was it the next day, and the next day. It seemed like over a week before people started to trickle back into the market place again. Lots of things changed. The price of food and other commodities increased instantly and tremendously. There was fear and panic in the atmosphere all the time. Our parents were glued to the radios listening to the latest news. Almost all the news that they did hear was fueled with fear.

There was a humorous news moment that I would never forget though. The radio announcer named, Okoko Ndem, stated that the bomb the enemies threw into the market place was incapable of killing a rat or a lizard, and that the plane almost crashed making the effort to throw this ineffective bomb. He mocked the enemy's miserable tactics, and lousy equipment. Well, I saw all the adults laughing for a change. They later gathered around the yard to compare notes. They did this regularly and it only produced more and more fear. The short wave radio was very popular at the time. I know my parents switched from the local news station to the British Broadcasting Corporation well known and abbreviated as BBC and sometimes they listened to Voice of America.

One day after one of these neighborhood heated discussions my father told my mother that she would have to leave town with us, their five children. "If there are check points and barricades here and there like they say, how do we get to leave?" she asked in hesitation. "We will make up a good story," he replied. "And this is it" he continued, Being a Barrister at the time, a journalist, and a Librarian, he was an expert in thinking up stories. "Our new born twins need medical treatment and have been referred to the specialist hospital near our hometown, Afipko. Since you are the homemaker you must take the other children with you. They will allow you and the children to pass. If I am with you they will not. Latter on I will act as if I have a

court case in our town and come join you, it is
a perfect plan, and it will work" he finished.
My mother had no choice in the matter but to
agree with it and we started to pack.

CHAPTER 2

Family

My father was a learned man. He spent nine years of his life, 1956 to 1965 in universities in England where he studied Law, Librarianship, and Journalism. Prior to his education in England he had attained a higher education in an institution called Hope Waddell Training Institute in Calabar of Cross River State in Nigeria where he also became a teacher. Hope Waddell is still a grand prominent institute of higher learning founded by some Presbyterian missionaries in the late 1800s. Teachers of those days were tough, non-tolerant of error, and I now understand why my father had the colossus ego he paraded around. No one could argue or cross him. He always had the first, middle, and the last word. He was very much older than my beautiful mother who he married at a young age of sixteen. My half brother and

He was much older than my beautiful mother who he married at a young age.

sister, Ezemba and Gertrude, were born to him in a previous short marriage to an Onitsha woman. Though with less education, they had the strong willed muscles needed to stand up to my father. They challenged his intellect all the time by challenging his common sense. "Common sense is not common" I would hear them say. There was consistent ragging fights between Ezemba and my father, or Gertrude and my father who both lived with us at the time in a huge home my father had rented from one of his acquaintances.

We also had two house boys who were distant relatives of my father, Sammy and Inya. My father was always punishing them for doing something wrong or not doing something right. My mother agonized witnessing his inhumane treatment of people. The fear of her speaking out against his rage was periodically dammed and replaced with righteous anger which was welcomed by all of us. The consequences were grave though, because he ended up pouring all his unrighteous indignation on her.

It sometimes resulted in her running away back home to her people and we, her children, left to the wolves. Either way it was never good. Our father had no peace within him, neither did he let anyone else around him have any. His intellectual self was only in his head; his heart was rock solid and his mind hardly seemed to be sober at leisure time that he was around us. As we grew up we acknowledged that we cannot emulate his character, or let any negative influences of it mold ours. We also came to terms that we could not have any of his money to make ourselves better. He was just a biological father, sad to say and a bitter truth to acknowledge, but that was it.

CHAPTER 3

The Journey Home

We had returned from England just two years earlier and had many nice things from abroad. They were all beautiful things to me. I had my favorite dolls, roller skates, educational toys of all kinds, a doll house and more. I tried to pack them all. My parents realized what I was doing and told me to leave those things because there will be no need for them. Well, the things did not mean anything to them, but they sure meant the whole world to me. I cried and begged my mother for my toys to be packed. I was too afraid to ask my father. She said that I can only take one doll and that my father has promised to bring all our belonging when he was coming. I had no choice but to believe her, so I did what I was told.

The news about the war progressing to our peaceful domain became more threatening.

We children stopped going to school as all schools were closed for safety's sake. We were not allowed to play in the yard or go into the streets like we used to. Life became dormant and uncertain. The atmosphere of peace and joy was overtaken by fear and terror. Anybody we did not know was a suspicious character and could be a lurking enemy planning to strike, destroy, and kill us.

We had to start being aware of our surroundings and environment which became more toxic itself with death stories. We were told that our water supply could be poisoned. Just before we were stopped from going to school, we were taught in school how to make charcoal masks which we were to put over our noses if the enemy attacked us at with any kind of gas bomb. We were also taught how to take cover in trenches and bunkers when the enemy came and attacked by 'air raids'. Well, not too long after those lessons did we get a chance to do the real thing. The enemy took note of its shortcomings from the radio broadcaster's mockery. This time they came back to this same little town with two war planes. Both on the same destructive mission but differently equipped. One was releasing bombs while the other scattered bullets all over the place. They were fast, swift, and fierce. We all thought we were prepared for this but the preparation was a mere joke.

The combination of the loud swift moves of two military jet planes, the explosions of the bombs and the shattering spray of bullets generated indescribable panic that overrode any thought of order. We all ran into the living room to get the twins. My mother grabbed the boy and our house help grabbed the girl. My mother screamed at me to go outside into the ditch or rather trench. Other people who watched us dig it ran towards it also. Before we could make it to the trench a plane came swerving by spraying bullets on its path. We all fell to the ground where we were and stayed there as if glued to it. One could hear screams and loud cries here and there. I thought we were all dead. The swift plane kept going back and forth. Large vibrating sounds, bullets sounds, crackling sounds followed their loud zooming moves back and forth in the air. After what seemed like forever, the sounds of the planes faded. Everywhere was still and quiet for quite a while. Suddenly I heard a voice say, "I think they are gone". The bushes started to rattle as people started to get up from their hiding places. Indigenes frantically called out names as they searched for their loved ones. It was a devastating reality.

The news on the radio this time was very sad and frightening. Many people died from that air raid. There was also a lot of destruction of residential dwellings and businesses. Everything shut down. No one went to their work or business. All supermarkets, food stores, open field markets were forced to close. The streets were deserted. Sadness, fear, and uncertainty ruled the communities and the atmosphere. The death toll was high, I cannot remember the exact number, but it was in the hundreds. Neither had this town nor this country experienced the death of people in such a great number in one day. Many who died in the market place were trampled on. Property destruction left a horrible memory and scars of the inhumane acts of wickedness; bombing and firing at civilian's homes, businesses, and open market places was an unforgiving atrocity.

The next day my father instantly made up his mind about our move out from Abakaliki. We completed our packing very quickly and hit the road. My father promised that he will come as soon as possible with as much of our belongings as he could bring. I believe my parents had chattered a station wagon Peugeot 404 that loaded all seven of us and our baggage, my mother, the five of us, her children, and our house maid.

There were so many check points on the way and my mother told the same story from one check point to another, and it worked. Each time the Biafran Military officer would ask if we were running away. My mother will answer, "No, my twin babies need medical checkup and care. We are taking them to the maternity hospital near our hometown for that reason" The Afipko Maternity Hospital had a great reputation for its superb medical care. They asked why we had so much stuff and my mother said she needed it for her other three children and her maid servant whom we were traveling with. The Biafran Military officer would then look into the car suspiciously but then let us go.

It was a very tense and slow journey. At each check point we wondered and worried that we might be turned back. Our worries were in vain since we made it to our home town safely and sound. My entire mother's relatives who were expecting us and were overjoyed to see us all arrive safely home and welcomed us over and over and over again, the warmest welcome I can remember receiving in my life.

CHAPTER 4

Life in Our Home Town

Life in Unwana, the name of our hometown, was quite different. My mother had a large warm and caring extended family. So many people heard of our arrival and came to say hello. They mostly liked to talk about the ongoing war, its atrocities, and the dim expectations.

Each person who visited hugged us, the children, and explained their relational ties with my family and how they helped change our diapers. As a child this confused me a lot because I knew that I spent my early childhood in England with a very loving Nanny whose name was Mrs. Moore and she changed our diapers. So many people who came around said the same thing; they either changed my diapers, my mother's, or my father's diapers. This must be a figure of speech meaning to know one so well, or from

34

the beginning of their lives, I thought because my father was older than some of the people saying this. I was right.

There was so much to learn and get used to. The way of life here was so different. We no longer had the privacy of our own rooms; there were no bathrooms, nor dining tables. Much seemed to be missing, yet people here laughed a lot. They were happy, very happy.

In our home town, we lived in a compound that my mother's great, great grandfather built for his big polygamous family. It consisted of a large main one story house of about three thousand square feet or more with six bed rooms, two living areas and a large long dark hallway. Both sides of the house were attached to mud brick walls forming a huge circle. In between the circled walls, were ten little mud huts that linked to each other with a little bit of the wall separating each house. A large gate led to the unpaved dusty street was always closed at about 7pm and locked at mid night. Each hut had a small back yard fenced in with braided palm tree branches knit tightly together.

Lots of things happened in these back yards. People bathed back there, stored food and seedlings back there, and even babies were born back there. It was a great opportunity and a valued enlightening experience for me to see how people in another part of this world lived their daily lives. It was very different from England and the bigger city we just moved from. In spite of the low standard of living, they seemed to be content with their lives and what they had.

Part of the town we lived was called Mission. This was a part of town secluded exclusively for Christians. The best homes were in this area and everyone was allowed to move freely. In the rest of the town were small villages with circular or rectangular hut like structures built in circles with a centered space of land in the middle. Each village had a large open land called Ogo with an open roofed building used for various purposes. Meetings were called at these points; huge wrestling matches were held and judged at these points. Village rituals of various kinds were made here regularly.

Before any kind of village activity started, an announcer passed through the small villages with warning information about the open village ritual space being closed or re-opened. Only the men who were initiated into the Ogo cult could pass through the Ogo when it was closed regardless of the number of hours or days it was closed.

Like a sponge, I soaked in quite a bit of knowledge and understanding. I also adapted quickly to my new environment. We heard less about the war except for the ongoing sounds of guns, grenades, and shelling that now sounded much further away. I did a lot of other things that kept me pre-occupied.

Some days I would go to the farms with my grandmother who we called Mma Jenny. Like many others who resided in the village, she was a full time farmer. She owned farm land in different places that yielded various kinds of crops. She went to different type of farm duties, most of which lasted all day or for days.

CHAPTER 5

The Farms

The Yam Tuber

One of the many valued farm crops till this day is the yam tuber. These are big heavy weight tubers beige on the inside with thick brown skin. The thick brown skin is not for consumption. The thick brown skin can be pealed before or after it is boiled in water to soften, then eaten with stew, vegetables, or dipped in seasoned palm oil. It can also be cooked as porridge yam in a beef stew like style. The peeled boiled yam can also be pounded in a large mortar with a long pestle into a type of dough called yam fufu which is hand molded into small round size balls then dipped into a tasty soup, stew, or source and then swallowed. This yam fufu dish is a very popular rich food eaten on special occasions or regularly by rich people who can afford it. The modern industry now has packaged yam powder which is easily poured into hot water and cooked into the yam fufu dough. The yam tuber is expensive, especially as it ages, and is always in high demand. Its value sets the traditional standard for wealth status in the Southeastern Region of the country.

A yam tuber has a head, body, and tail section to it. The tail and head sections are sometimes bitter especially if the crop is new or very aged. The body part is the best part for consumption. It can have a nice sweet taste and is very filling. The head of a mature yam is the seedling and can survive for years if stored tied horizontally above the ground in barns. The older the seedling, the better and bigger the yam crop harvests. Rich farmers have huge barns of yam seedlings ageing on acres of land. The bigger the barn the wealthier the owner is determined to be.

We went to a yam farm to prepare the grounds for the yam seedlings. Big muscle toned men were hired to till numerous huge upside down cone shaped heaps of soil on acres of land. It was physical hard labor to observe. With giant size hoes, they piled up soil upon soil to shape numerous upsides down cones of soil.

A Lot of cassava fufu with vegetable soup was the dish prepared by my grandmother and her maid servants to feed these tough hard workers. I watched as they took their break and settled under a large tree shade close to where I was. They washed their hands with water provided for them in calabash like containers, without any soap.

They ate hungrily with both hands and completely finished the food, then drank a lot of water, relaxed under the shade for about half an hour telling stories of village life to one another with laughter and joy that proceeded from merry hearts. They argued about stuff I did not understand in loud voices, but ended up in laughter. They would then return to work re-energized till dawn. They completed the designated farmland before they stopped tilling, packed up, and then went home. I guess they precisely pre-sized the job to know how many of them could finish it within the time designated. They were paid their wages and said they were hired for another farm the next day.

I had come to the farm with my grandmother's wrapping cloth and a thin nicely woven colorful mat. I had used the cloth to tie my baby doll on my back like I saw women in the village carry their babies. When I got to the farm I tied the four edges of the cloth to four shrubs making a temporary shade, then I put the mat underneath. It was a nice picnic like shade and I was comfortable there most of the time. My grandma would join me there from time to time for a chat or ask if I was alright. My doll had a comfortable position, and was my constant companion, so I was satisfied. When the ground tillers had finished their work, it was time for all of us to go.

We first went to a close-by stream and bathed, we also got some drinking water from a very clean and cool spring called "Ochighaighai" and then headed home. Ochighaighai is a well-known spring that is trusted for its cleanness and coolness. Its cold water slowly seeps out of the rocks. Even in the hot sunny seasons it retains its coolness just like iced water. Women and children frequent this faraway spring with round clay potteries called "Ite Mini" and stored the drinking water in a larger clay pottery called "Adu" which kept the water cool inside a corner in the house. The Adu pottery continuously released a refreshing earth taste until the water finished.

On coming into the town, on our way home, we started to receive greetings from just about everyone we passed. Every home we passed shouted out welcome and well done greetings as well. The warmest, was always when we walked into our own compound, anyone around or in the compound ran out to greet us and help take the load off our heads as they showered us with more encouragement and well done greetings.

Later in the evening, after some nice hot food, we rested in the middle of the compound on nice hand woven mats under the glowing moon light. It was beautiful, warm, and cozy, especially when the full moon was out. So many children and adults will come out of their houses and gather around to tell folk stories.

The folk stories were always interesting and everyone was attentive. The adults will tell the children and each other one story after another; some of them had songs with choruses which we all responded to with joy, while some stories were sad with tragic endings. We listened to those in tears and went to bed in sadness after hearing the tragedies, but the unity of these moments were memorable, bonding, and priceless.

How the tortoise got its rough shell was one of the most popular stories we heard over and over in different versions. The story teller will start off shouting a loud word, "Otee!" This would get the attention, interest, and curiosity of everyone. All who heard that word shouted out will know that the story teller is about to begin. All who wanted to hear will gather close to take a sitting position close to the story teller's side and respond, "Oyor!" The story teller will repeat this many times until everyone is situated and attentive. It is just like saying "Once upon a time".

This story began with hunger and famine in the land of the animals, but the birds got an invitation to come to a special place in the sky for an overnight feast. Tortoise heard about it and asked the birds if he could come along. They said he could if only he could fly, but since he did not have wings he could not.

Tortoise then asked for their help in making him wings. The kind birds being curious asked how they could help. Tortoise said if each bird would contribute a feather, they would not miss it and he can get two luxurious wings, and then he too could fly up with them. The birds talked about it and agreed, so tortoise got his wings.

As they were about to set off to the feast, tortoise came up with another idea, that they should all take a special name for the occasion. The unsuspecting birds were not aware of tortoise's cunning character, and they all agreed with him and took a name. He took his name last as "All of You". They then took off and flew to the feast. The host was very pleased with them for honoring his invitation and had prepared a dainty bountiful dinner and presented it before them. As he was about to exit the room tortoise stopped and asked him who it was for and he replied "Oh! It's for all of you" Tortoise then grinned at the birds as he greedily started eating the food as he shouted with joy "It's for all of you, that's me!" The birds were shocked, and had no choice but to eat the crummy leftovers turtle had messed up and felt for them.

The next morning, it was the same with the last meal. So after they finished each bird took their feather away from tortoise's wings. He begged the birds for a last favor since he couldn't fly but had to go back to earth. They agreed to tell tortoise's wife to put out all the mattresses, pillows, cushions, and soft materials so he can free fall onto them and not be hurt. When the birds got to earth, they chose to play tortoise's cunning game, so they told his wife that tortoise instructed her to put out pots, pans, knives, machetes, and all hard material and she did. When tortoise called out to ask if all was set, "Yes!" she replied back with an assuring shout. So tortoise free fell into the hard surfaces and his shell was all broken up. His wife helped him patch up his broken shell back into one and placed it back on his back. That is how the tortoise got his cracked up back shell. The story teller then ends it with the same "Otee!" requiring the listeners' chorus, "Oyọr!" If any other person had a story to tell, they would make the call for continued attention and engagement.

Such stories were also an ingenious way of instilling virtue and good moral values into the minds of the younger generations. To know right and wrong was and still is an important family value. The consequences of wrong choices were emphasized in the stories as much as the rewards of making the right ones. Sometimes we fell asleep in the middle of a story. At a certain time the adults would also give up and call it a day or a night. The little ones were carried to their sleeping places and the young adults were walked to theirs with a guiding hand.

The warmest thing about the village life was the shared love. There was a lot of love and care for one another. Everyone looked out for the others' children and kept each other in check and accountable for one another's daily life and behavior. It was comforting and sheltering.

If a child was caught doing any wrong deeds an older person around had the right to correct them on the spot and report them to their family. Any member of the family can discipline that child. All young adults and adults are accountable for their deeds to other members of the family. Family meetings were held regularly and all disputes and problems presented and resolved without delay. Any stubborn adult who thought they were above correction would later hear their names in caricatured songs composed by observant and nosy villagers, and then sang by all. The mockery and shame that individual and their entire family had to endure was enormous and cemented a tarnished image and reputation for life. This was one of the reasons for early family interventions of problems and customary need for proper child upbringing. There were also songs of praise and exultation for heroic characters as well. It took the whole village to raise the children.

The Harmattan Season

During December Christmas holiday season, the weather in this region becomes extremely dry with dusty West African trade wind which blows south from the Sahara desert. It is called the Harmattan season and lasts for about 3 months.

The Cross River borders our state, East Central State with Cross River State. The Cross River loses some of its water volume, so large sand beds emerged in the middle creating sand islands we call "Etta". During one of our folk story nights we were told another true story about the water elephant that terrorized the river bay visitors and merchants who made their living within the surrounding environment. It prevented the boat trade, fishing expeditions, fun that went on at the river surroundings, and the Etta picnics. It killed a lot of people who visited Etta, but one day a hunter, named Okonkwo, determined to put an end to the river bank's chaos took his machete and headed to the river. He waited for hours until the water elephant emerged. They charged at each other. Even though the water elephant was a big strong animal, Okonkwo known as a tactful brave hunter, overpowered it and cut off its head with his sharpened long machete. He went back to the village with the animal's head in his hand dripping with its blood. People rejoiced and celebrated the freedom from its terror for seven joyous days and honored him with a chieftaincy title called "Ogbu Enyi," meaning elephant killer. He became famous and his name was used to sing songs that everyone sang, especially at happy times. Somehow, both famous and infamous people were remembered for things they had done in songs and stories that were passed on from generation to generation.

The next day my grandmother took another crew to the same farm we went to days before. This time, women came with basins on their heads and little hoes. They first went into the backyard where our family had a small barn of ageing yam seedlings and loaded up their basins with them. It was very early and the morning was still dark.

When they got to the farm, each lady took different sections of the farm, dug the soft soil at the top of the upside down cone the men had made previously, and put a yam seedling in as deep as they could, marked the cone with a long sturdy bamboo stick that they put in the middle of the cone and moved onto the next one. The yam vine has to grow upwards on the bamboo stick for the tube to obtain its optimal health and the farmer in turn, a good harvest. They diligently worked until all the cones were completed and all yam seedlings were planted. At about midday they were finished. My grandma paid them their wages and we again headed to that nearby stream where we drank some nice clean cold water, and bathed in the stream, and then headed to another farm.

This was a vegetable farm where she planted okra, ground nuts also known as peanuts, peppers, and some other vegetables. She used the little hoe to loosen the soil around the smaller upside down cone, then used her left bare hand to gather and pull a bunch of weeds from the ground with their roots. She shook them over the upside down cones, and then tossed the weed in a bundle, which she later gathered and moved to a side of the farm to degrade and then used back as manure. She gently and coherently worked around the crops. She was fast and efficient. It was interesting to see how easy she made the work seem. I took the spare hoe she had in her

The yam vine has to grow upwards on the bamboo stick for the tube to obtain its optimal health.

A small barn of ageing yam seedlings

basin and did some, then realized it was a lot of hard work. I did a few cones and went back to my shade.

I was really glad that I was not obligated to do this. I did not want to earn my wages this way, I thought. In about two hours she had finished weeding this acre of farm. We then went to a different stream, washed up, got some water and then we went home.

The Cassava root

The cassava farm was also interesting and my grandmother had more than one of those too. This tuber is small compared to the yam, and very different in nature. Although it looks like a tubule, it is actually called the cassava root. It grows a tall thin stem with leaves that fall off as it grows, leaving mostly fresh leaves at the top of the long stem with very few or no branches.

At about the third to fourth month after planting, the cassava crop matures for harvest. My grandma would go to the cassava farm with a small hoe and a sharp machete a large empty basin, food, snacks, and a small calabash with drinking water. We got to this farm as early as 6:00 am and she went right to work.

The layout of the farm was the same as the vegetable farm with small upside down like soil cones. She would hold onto the long cassava stem and pull it. With that firm pull each stem will release three to four tubers of cassava. Each cone had three to four stems. She therefore had quite a harvest from one cone. When she was finished pulling the stems from a soil cone, she would build the cone back up, take the cassava stems in twos, cut them up into about six inch pieces and replanted them in twos back into the soil cone where she removed the root tubules from. Some soil cones had three sets, and some had four.

It looked too laborious, so I settled for chopping up the stems and laying them handy for her. That was work enough. By the time we had finished a third of the farm, we had quite a bit of cassava root piled up from out of the ground. I knew it would not fit into the basin she had. She needed to make several trips home to get them all. As I was going to ask how we were going to get all this home, one of the young ladies that lived in our compound came to the farm with another lady. They hugged and talked a bit, then got to the business at hand. My grandma removed some cassava from the heap, put it to the side and gave them a price. They bargained back and forth for a while. My grandma then added a few tubes to the small pile. The young ladies then untied their wraps and deep down into their waist were long cloths made into belts. In turns, they unfolded their belts and there were their banks. They each paid cash for the cassava they bought and my grandma in turn

Although it looks like a tubule,
it is actually called
Cassava Root.

untied her bank belt hidden deep inside her waist and added her earned money to what she already had, and then secured it back in its place. They both took some tubes and we all headed to another stream.

There was a slight stench which grew stronger as we approached this stream. When we got there it was amazing to see cut up cassava tubes fermenting by the sides of this slow running water. There were various objects that marked ownership. It was remarkable to know that no one took or stole from the other's inventory left in this nearby stream for days.

My grandma took a perforated calabash that lay beside a fermented set of cut up cassava, and then she put it in a raffia bag and started to sieve the fermented cassava through the calabash into the bag. She threw the skin and roughage into the water. When she was done sieving the fermented batch, she cut up the fresh ones she brought into about four inch size cylinder like shapes and replaced the old ones. She left her perforated calabash on top of it just like it was when we got there, then took the raffia bag, hauled it on top of a large stone, and squeezed out as much water as she could. There was a considerable amount of concentrated fermented cassava in the now smaller bag. Still wet and drippy, she put it in her basin and we headed back to the farm. The young ladies, who had bought cassava from my grandmother, had done the same thing.

When we got back to the farm, grandma loaded the rest of the cassava tubers into her basin, and we went home. It looked all profitable for a day's work. She had harvested, planted, and traded. Now we were going home with some processed food, ready to be cooked as another fufu style dish and some money.

Cassava is a very popular tubule or root that is processed in various ways. The fermented type described above is popular in

Eastern Nigeria. At a certain consistency, the starchy mix is put in a pot, and then heated slowly, turning it into a transparent smooth dough. This is another form of fufu that swallows smoothly down the throat and eaten with the favorite "nsala" and "Iyaya" soups or any other one of the numerous types of soups.

Gari

The most popular fufu type is gari. This is sold all over West Africa. Gari keeps the cassava root in high demand. The local method of producing gari is long and tedious. Cassava root are brought home in basins. We all gathered around with knives to peel off the thick brown skin and the immediate layer underneath the outer brown skin. When all the skin is off, the cassava is then thoroughly washed. After this, women would place long handmade graters over a large wide basin, sit on one side and then grate the cassava roots in twos or threes at a time into the basin until it is all done.

The grated cassava is then loaded into raffia bags, and the two to three day drying process then begins. The ends of two large long sticks are laid on top of four large stones that keep them off the ground. The sticks are laid parallel to each other with a two to three feet gap, depending on how big the raffia bag is. Smaller, but strong sticks are laid across the two big sticks in the middle part of them. The opening to the raffia bag is tied firm with a two or three braided rope and then laid across the smaller sticks. Another set of small sticks are then laid on top of the raffia bag parallel to the smaller sticks below it. Two large long sticks are then laid on top of the small sticks, parallel to the two large sticks at the bottom on the four stones. A strong two or three braided rope is then used to tie the ends of the bottom large sticks to the top large sticks individually at the four corners thereby putting pressure on the small sticks which in turn squeezes on the raffia bag, causing water to be pressed out of the grated cassava. Once the tie is firm and tight the whole thing is lifted off the ground and placed vertically to keep it off the ground to prevent sand and other contaminants from getting into it. As the water drains out, the four ropes at the four ends are periodically tightened to keep it draining until all water is out. It is critical to get the water drained as fast as possible. Any residue of water left in the grated cassava can cause it to degrade or mold and ruin the whole lot of grated cassava. After about two days it becomes impossible to squeeze any more liquid out of the bag. The bag is then opened and a bit of the compacted grated cassava is laid on a fine sieve and rubbed in a circular motion through the sieve. Fine particles come through and sprinkle into a container placed underneath the fine sieve. The fine white granules signals as a green light confirming the drying process to be complete and the sieving and frying process could then start.

The entire raffia bag of dried grated cassava is then sieved little by little into a basin. Once a considerable amount is in the basin, a fire is prepared. Logs of wood are placed in-between three large stones of the same size, set close together in a triangular setting. Kerosene is poured in the middle where the logs meet and a match lit and thrown into it. As the wood begins to burn, a large round open iron pan is placed on the three stones above the fire and heated. A table spoon full of palm oil is put in the hot pan and a small amount of grated cassava is poured over the simmering oil and blended in. The palm oil instantly turns the white cassava color to red. More grated cassava is heaped into the heated pan with a piece of calabash which is shaped to scoop and evenly steer the grated cassava around the large open iron pan. The color lightens to a light orange color as the cassava granules gradually dries into a fine finished product called gari. Without the oil it is called white gari. More palm oil causes it to be more yellow or yellowish red.

Gari is made into fufu dough by steering it into hot boiled water and left to set and cool for a few minutes. It can then be rolled into little balls, dipped in various soups prepared especially for eating fufu, and then swallowed. The poor, who cannot afford the ingredients used to make soup, pour cold water into gari with a pinch of salt, peanuts, or sugar and eat it like cereal most of the time.

Gari is a great commodity in all African markets and is measured with open milk cans, calabashes, raffia bags, or other packaging of various sizes. The finest gari sells the quickest. Some crooked traders who do not have fine looking gari will buy fine looking gari and sprinkle over the bad one and display it as good instead of reducing the price to get rid of it. Some put paper and other kinds of fillers or toppers in their measuring cups to deceive buyers with unjust measuring scales.

My grandmother taught me a lot about the pros and cons of trading in order to avoid the cons and embrace the pros. If we were out of gari and had to buy, she would dig her hand deep into the basin or bag and pull out the inner granules, if it was consistent with the outer ones, then she will ask for the measuring cup and check it out before bargaining down the price. She was a great honest merchant herself with God fearing values. My grandmother was hardworking, transparent, meek, and wise. I did not understand then, but I appreciate her much more now that she has gone home to be with the Lord.

CHAPTER 6

The New Yam Festival

We had now been back in our home town for over six months. We started to get used to village life and also adapted to our grandparent's old environment. Most young adults leave the village to go to the townships or larger cities to school and work since farming and trading were the main professions in the village, but with the war in progress the village was believed to be the safest place to live, therefore many who lived in the towns and other states were all home seeking refuge.

Time was warming up to the upcoming New Yam Festival. As I said before, yam in the whole Eastern Region also known as the Ibo Land, was and still is a big deal. In our hometown, its harvesting festival is called "Iri Ji". As the planted yam matures for harvest, it is considered new yam and no one eats any of it prior to the date designated for the "Iri Ji" ceremony, which lasts about three to seven days. It is symbolized as a Thanksgiving holiday period to God for blessing the crops and giving His people harvest. Many come home to be with their families to celebrate the Iri Ji festival.

Christians praise, worship, and thank God Almighty for their harvest while non-Christians thank their village idols. The harvested yam is cooked in different ways and eaten with gratitude to God and a lot of merry making. There is the yam fufu dough style already mentioned, the yam porridge dish in the style of beef stew with yam, boiled yam and separate stew dish style, fried yam and stew dish style, roasted yam and palm oil style. These were and continue to be the various ways of eating and feasting with the new yam. This yam cannot be eaten uncooked or under cooked because it has an itching element that can cause serious allergies to the throat and many times when it touches the skin.

A lot of visitors enjoy these festive times with villagers. Visits are made from house to house without any kind of formal invitations or protocol. The various yam dishes are served and consumed with gratitude to God, the farmers, cooks, and other contributors for making the harvest a success. Freedom floats in the air turning the atmosphere into cherished joyous and generous moments that are stored up in the psychic for memorable future joyous recall.

Another Air Raid

As the joyous atmosphere was settling, a hard time moved right in on top of it. On a warm late Sunday morning, after a nice and inspiring service at our local Presbyterian Church, as we were relaxed at home, we heard the sound of a low flying plane. It was not swift nor was it too slow. The loud noise due to its closeness to the ground brought us all

I ran as fast as my little legs could carry me towards a huge umbrella like tree.

out of our houses.

To our greatest surprise there was a big blast that seemed to shake the universe. With panic and fear people ran screaming for all to take cover because it was the enemies' war plane. We heard explosion and vibrations after explosion and more vibrations. I ran as fast as my little legs could carry me towards a huge umbrella like tree that was across the dusty unpaved street from where we lived. I dived underneath it hoping that its thick branches and wide leaves would hide me from the plane's view.

The sounds of the continued bombing was so terrifying that it seemed to be right on my very own head which I covered with my hands as I laid face down on the bare dusty ground praying for it to go away. It was indescribably awful. After what seemed like forever the bombing stopped. Someone came and lifted me up. As I rose out of the mini shock mode, I realized I was still alive and that what had just happened was real.

Many people had sought refuge under this huge unique tree. Family members called out for one another. I ran home to find out what happened to my family and gave account of myself. It was not till later on in the evening that every one of our family members was accounted for. Again things changed. Our small hometown was no longer the safe haven we thought it to be. Also being the hometown of a prominent former Governor of the eastern region of Nigeria, Ezeogo Dr. Akanu Ibiam then known as Sir Frances Akanu Ibiam, made it unsafe for us all. Little did we know that his prominent status made our small hometown a prime target of the enemy who attacked us with two bomber planes at the same time. No one expected what happened. The report stated that eleven bombs were dropped altogether, but only four caused damage. Two bombs were thrown at Chief Akanu Ibiam's compound; one partially hit his compound while some hit the valley his home overlooked and blew up there. Three were dropped into the school and damaged part of the school structure while the others scattered. There were casualties from flying debris, but no fatalities were reported.

The next day the Biafran government provided anti-aircraft machineries to detour any such future attacks. All that was too late, the damage had been done in the minds of the people. They did not trust that protection and deserted the town for the farms very early the next morning. For the next few months or so, that became the new routine of life for most of our people, leave for the farms at dusk and return to the village at dawn. We were all eager to leave. Fear and uncertainty griped the whole communities. The sounds of guns, shelling, and grenades grew stronger and louder; an indication that the war frontline was getting closer. The walls of the house we lived shook from the vibration and debris kept

Ezeogo Dr. Akanu Ibiam,
then known as Sir Frances Akanu Ibiam.

clattering from the weak structures. Most of the so called good homes were built with mud brick then lightly coated with cement. They were very old, probably built in the late eighteen hundreds or early nineteen hundreds and the walls were now weak, cracking, and failing at every vibrating shake.

Adults always gathered to hear and tell the latest of the war developments. No one we knew owed a television at the time. Short wave radios were still the best means of getting information, while letters and word of mouth were the others.

CHAPTER 7

The Exodus

The sound of shelling, bombing, and bullet spray became heavier, day and night. I recall staying tensely awake all night listening to the exchange of the various ammunition sounds. The bullets would spray, and then spray again, and then a shell would drop. Another type of bullet will spray, again, again and again, and then a grenade will blast. Then a shelling will blast, blast again, then a grenade will blast, in turn falling debris will rattle from the ceiling of our domain to the ground. Night after night, day after day, the same damming sounds that stored terror and fear in the minds of both great and small. I sure did think I was the only one who stayed awake and absorbed the war's amore music since no one spoke up, but one day my siblings and cousins reassured that I was not the only one. Early that morning, one of my older cousins,

Udu said, "Wow! It seems like they are right next door" and others assured they were awake by responding in agreement.

That same morning, we were all packed up to go to the farms when one of my uncles we called, Bro Richie, returned from a short trip from the neighboring town where my father was staying. He confirmed our fears. "The enemy has invaded the neighboring village, so they are right next door" my father said echoing our early morning conversation. My father had finally come with my uncle.

My father never came back to live with us; neither did he bring any of our belongings like he promised. My mother told me that he had left the town we used to live in and was living in the neighboring town because business was more favorable there. They came with bad news and with genuine worry in their voices they stated that we could not go to the farms. The rebels were too close and that

Our large family and extended family of about thirty five people packed up and headed on a long tedious foot journey miles away from the home we all knew.

we only had a day or so ahead of them to move to another place of safety and stay ahead of them.

The whole family retreated back into the house to talk. The talks and plans were very brief. The rebels were approaching very rapidly from the east. We were to pack up as much stuff as we could carry on our heads and start walking to the neighboring village towards our west which was opposite to their advancement.

Our large family and extended family of about thirty five people packed up and headed on a long tedious foot journey miles away from the home we all knew. There was a lot of grief, sadness, and worry of the uncertainty of our future. We only had one little black car. I cannot remember what type of car it was or who it belonged to. It was used to make trips to take some of our belongings out to where we were heading. I so badly wished I could get a ride and not have to suffer so much walking for so long. We not only had to walk so long, but to do so without shoes. I had outgrown all my shoes. Our feet hurt and were blistered walking on those stony rough dusty roads. We became hungry, thirsty, and weary from the long tedious journey. There were so many of us and little food to go around. Again my father was no were to be found. It was my mother and her extended family that cared for our entire well-being to the best that they could. Many were very sympathetic to us having come back from England to suffer so much of an ordeal and enormous hardship. Desperate and favorable efforts were made to feed us; I mean my mother and her five children.

At a certain point we were told of a nearby stream of clean cool water, but first we temporarily stayed in an open school building. We went with the first group to the stream, drank nice cool clean water to our heart's content, bathed and swam for a long time, and then returned and I fell asleep. Exhausted from the journey and with the sound of the threat of war a little further away I was able to fall into a deep sweet sleep again.

We, the children, were awakened the next morning to go and fetch some more water for food to be made. We did and after that needed meal we all washed up and continued on the journey away from home. Later that evening we arrived at a village called Ebu-Unwana where my family had some extended relatives. We spent about five days there waiting for the return of our men who had gone to find a safer place for us to settle.

CHAPTER 8

Home Away From Home
Olokoro Umuahia

We ended up on the back of a big open truck normally used to carry and deliver sand, which took us to a small town called Olokoro in Umuahia. One of my aunties and her family lived and worked in this town, so they graciously allowed us all to squat in their home for a few days, after which my mother and uncles found and rented a big compound with lots of room. We settled in different rooms according to family ties, similar to how we lived in the village back home. Temporarily, we were one big happy family again, though miles away from home, but glad to be together and away from the war zones. The environment was different. Again life changed. No more farms for my grandmother and I. Things were now done differently, very differently.

We all added a year to our ages in this small town located in the outskirts of Umuahia. With no school or much work, we just idled away the abundance of time we had. It was as if we had forty eight hours in a day instead of twenty four. We took numerous trips to the streams to fetch water since the water faucets in the house we lived in never dripped.

The pathway to the popular stream we frequented was wide enough to drive cars through it, but had rocks of various sizes that stuck out of the grounds. We had to control our walk down the steep sloppy broad pathway which caused our strides to be briskly and we often dashed our feet against the stones. As a toe hit the rock skin would peal open, then pain and blood would compete with each other. Whenever this happened to anyone we would all stop to help the wounded one. The first aid was to take the peeled off skin, which was usually hanging, and put back over the cut open flesh, and then put pressure for it to glue back on and stop the bleeding, but the wounded had to endure the pain until it subsided. However, the wounded one would still limp on to the stream and complete the chore. Sometimes it happened going uphill of which we would abruptly drop the containers of water from our heads spilling the water. In this case, the individual had to limp back to the stream to replenish their water without the company of the others. This was a painful and suffering experience that wore out our slippers and feet, but was not life threatening.

There was a military anti-aircraft set up nicely tucked away from sky and street view inside the bushes off of this same pathway. The young military guys would come out frequently to walk around and go to the stream to bathe and fetch water too. With all the time we had on our hands and the adults gone to do one kind of work or another no one questioned our whereabouts during the day. We were free as birds without clipped wings.

One of my mother's second young cousins, a few years older than me got involved with one of those military guys. She always wanted to go and fetch water, and she called me to go with her. We would detour into the bushes where the anti-aircraft set up was stationed, then she'd ask me to wait at a certain spot, and then she disappeared for a long time. I was very afraid for her and myself. Sometimes my wait would be so long and I would wonder what was going on and if something had happened to her. On one occasion I had started to leave in order to go get an adult when I heard her call out to me because I had moved from the spot where I was supposed to be. I hurried back to see her standing with one of the military guys that I saw regularly at the stream. I stood there in shock and doubt as to what I was thinking. He whispered something into her ears and she giggled and left him to meet me. "Come on lets go" she said, without an apology or any sense of guilt. I followed her behind and seeing her back, with some dead grass and other debris stuck on her clothes, hair and skin. This confirmed my suspicion as to what she was doing in the bushes. From that day on I refused to go with her. She did not like me very much afterwards, but she found another escort to the stream. I did not tell anyone, but kept it to myself.

Our mother and many other adults from our family went to work in the busy township of Umuahia. She had attained an associate degree in domestic science from a junior college in England and was excellent in preparing certain dishes, bakery, and pastries. They teamed up with other relatives and opened up a canteen that was very successful at the time. It provided some members of the family with work and all of us with good tasting delicious leftover food any day they went to cook. They served breakfast and lunch. We always looked forward to their return home to get the delicious leftover food that also included bread and pastries. My voiced desire to go to the township with them was always refused by my mother, stating that it was too dangerous. So we stayed back and ran all the errands and chores that were assigned to us. Any child that was asked to do anything always had a joyful companion. As long as the air raids stayed away, and the shelling and gun fight sounds stayed at a distance, we children were all fine and joyous.

In the evenings we all sat around and composed and sang war songs. In most of the songs we asked God to kill and defeat the enemy. Some of them would list all the saboteurs who betrayed our new country, Biafra, for financial gain and we sang to God to punish them with death. We also sang songs to God to stop or end the war with victory for us so that we could go back to the homeland that He blessed us with. We composed so many songs, some of which we remember till this day. Every evening was a routine. We would all gather in the middle of the compound and sing one war winning song after another till late night. If the songs could kill our enemies, they would have been all dead and victory would have been ours even before the war started, but it was not so. I guess as we sang the enemy sang too. Most of the children will fall asleep on the mat. The young ones were carried in and we were awakened and led into the house. We children were usually left to sleep as much as we wanted into the late morning.

One morning, after the adults had all left for work, we were abruptly awakened by the anti-aircraft siren warning of approaching air raids. As we ran to take cover, that overwhelming terror sound zoomed by. Again, the swift loud sound of a vicious fighter aircraft tearing through the skies and spraying bullets everywhere in its paths, the siren warning was like a bad joke. The aircrafts raged its way back and forth while its target seemed to be the township where my mother and the rest of my family worked at, Umuahia.

Suddenly, there was another one emptying its ammunition on another section of the same town. Sometimes they would both zoom their way back right over our heads and disappeared just as fast. The anti-aircraft stationed on our way to the stream fired nonstop when they came within range. It was indescribably frightening. Everyone lost all sense of control and ran aimlessly to wherever seemed safer than where they were. Again what seemed like forever suddenly stopped and all went quiet. I found myself far in a wooded area in the back yard, conscious but overridden and consumed with fear. A lot of other people hid themselves there too. So many of us were bleeding from wounds we sustained from the harsh bushes, sticks, and thistles that ripped and tore on our skin while running for shelter.

I don't recall having gone to the hospital, but I do recall how terrified I was as to what the fate of my mother and the rest of our family were since the air raid centered in their work area. We gathered back together and my grandfather who was always around brought the radio. We listened in tears and sobs as the radio announcer described the genocide heaped on our people. He announced the areas that were hard hits and the devastation the air raid had caused. I was terribly weakened to the point that I could no longer stand. I fell to the ground and threw up a lot of bitter gall. The thought of my mother not coming back was one that I could not bear. She was everything to me, to us. She was my mother and my father to us. She cared for us and loved us. She sacrificed for us and protected us with unconditional love. Our father was somewhere in that same town and did not care whether we lived or died, but my mother did. "If anything happened to her I will not forgive the people who caused this war", I thought.

As I lay on the floor with these horrible and sickening thoughts and half-conscious I felt myself slipping into oblivion, but someone called me, vigorously shook me, and then poured some cold water on me. The cold water did it. My eyes opened. I heard my grandfather ask them to take me into the house. I was carried in and I fell into a deep sleep, no dreams.

Later I was awakened by shouts and loud noises. I got up and ran out to find my mother and her team all back. I also screamed and shouted for joy. No one could tell how joyful I was. I could not express my joy and relief to anyone. No one would understand the weight that fell off from my shoulders at the sight of my mother, alive. They all looked so roughened up and some had open wounds on them too, lots of wounds. Their stories were worse than ours and much more terrifying.

They were in the middle of the whole chaos and witnessed the air strikes. All targets were civilian strikes, they said, and all the civil servants working poured out into the streets desperately looking for trees or large shrubs to hide underneath. Young working class women in running for their lives kicked off their high heel shoes and ripped their tight knee skirts. They were all calm now to joke and laugh about the horrible experience.

It happened in the late morning. They cooked, and just started to serve lunch in the canteen, but since the airstrikes interrupted them, they brought all the food back. Oh gosh, was it a lot of food! Good stuff; lots of meat pies, different type of soups, various rice dishes, meats, to mention but a few. They did not go back to work for a few days. The food was preserved by periodically warming it on burning fire generated by dried wood. The meat pie we had to eat up as soon as possible. There were neither refrigerators nor electricity to help preserve any of it.

As things went back to normal they resumed work. I do not know how much their loss was from all that setback, all I know is that the Almighty God continued to provide through their hard work at the canteen for the duration of time we lived in that town.

Our Earthly Father

One day my mother returned from their long tedious day at the canteen and told us she found out where my father was staying. She had gotten a message that he was very sick to the point of death. My dear late uncle Richie made the needed arrangement to go with her to see him. "How long are you going to stay?" I asked. "We do not know, two days or so. We will come back as soon as we can." "Here we go again!" I thought. I hated it when my mother had to be away out of my sight; and leaving for some days, that was very troubling to me. The thought of waiting and hoping for her to come back threatened to wreck my young nerves. The first day seemed like a year, and the second day like a century, the third day I sat outside waiting until dawn. I went to bed. When I woke up in the morning they were back.

They had a tedious trip. When they got to the house my father was living, they met a woman whom claimed to be my father's wife. My uncle then introduced her to the real wife and asked for his where about. She wrote down the hospital name and address where he was and gave it to them, and they left to go look for him at the hospital.

When they got to the hospital and visited him, he was out of intensive care and would live, the nurses reported. My mother and uncle then wished him well and left. On their way home the tires to the borrowed motor cycle they rode on busted, both tires and the inner tubes, because of the rough roads. There was no place to repair or replace the tires, so they continued the rough bumpy ride home on the tireless vehicle. It got dark, the roads were unsafe with stones and potholes, and this petrified my mother, but my uncle encouraged her and the good Lord brought them home, though very sour and in a lot of physical and emotional pain, but safe.

Her marriage to my father was over, concluded my uncle, and he encouraged my mother to move on. He promised her that she had her family's backing, and she always did. God blessed her, and directed her path, she then became the bread winner who kept her children, parents, and extended family fed, clothed, and united all throughout the war time.

We were one big happy extended family. Every one helped in one way or another. My grandmother cared for my twin brother and sister. I helped care for them too, especially when my grandmother went to the markets to trade and make money. I loved to cook the special dishes and feed them because I ate some too.

Our home environment was much better than when we lived with my father. There was always trouble, sorrow, and fear around him. He would go out in the evenings and come home drunk. He talked loud and beat up people, including my mother who sometimes ran away back to her people. It was like war at home with one unpleasant incident after another. We were left to the mercy of our house boys and our half-sister. She was cruel to us at times. The house we lived in was big and very lonely without my mother and I dreaded her absence then and dreaded her absence at this war time too.

I prayed to have a better husband than my father was to my mother and a better father to his children than my father was to us. Being with my mother's family was like what I hear of heaven. They were peaceful and loving, especially when comparing it to what we had. Everyone looked out for the other and loved one another. It was so easy to do stuff and complete tasks. The irony of it was the peace we felt within in spite of the turmoil of war around.

Mother and Her Extended Family

My grandparents were God fearing people. They prayed a lot and sang praises to God from the Ancient and Modern hymns. Back home we attended the Presbyterian Church, which was the only church we had in our hometown. The Presbyterian Church was introduced by young white missionaries who came from England in the late 1800s. They labored the mosquito infested environment, installed churches and made disciples who worked with them to establish, nurture, and grow the churches. Some of them died young from malaria and were buried there in our hometown. They were honorably laid to rest with marble tombstones engraved with their names, date, age, and cause of death highlighting their memorial.

At the time my mother was not a fanatic in Jesus Christ as my grandparents were. So, I believe that she lived and benefited off the dividends of their prayers till she found Christ Jesus for herself. I also believe that the peace of God was with her family and always will be because of the deep rooted and grounded love relationship my grandparents had with Jesus Christ. Mother later picked up on that and followed in my grandmother's footsteps.

All young men of families who were eighteen years or older were all out fighting with the Biafran military, including my mother's younger brother, Isaac, and many of her cousins. They joined Biafran military as volunteers at the very beginning of the declaration of the Nigerian and Biafran war. Some attained high ranking military status that privileged them to have "back men" generally known as personal bodyguards.

My mother's younger sister, Nkechi, was pledged to be married to a Biafran Lieutenant named Nnanna. He was a jovial, generous, handsome young man. We all loved him. He played with us and brought a lot of goodies when he came to visit. He also had a "back man" who stayed by, settled at a distance and watchful since there was no eminent danger. He spent the weekend and then they left.

A few weeks later, his 'back man' came back with news of his death. The military had already laid him to rest. My aunty, his fiancée was devastated and sobbed uncontrollably on and off for weeks. We were all saddened and cried profusely as well. We eulogized him in our daily conversation and cherished his last visit. That was the best we could all do.

CHAPTER 9

Another Exodus

We never seemed to know what day of the week or month of the year it was and did not really care. Day after day life was a routine. Air raids came, shook us up and left. The distant regular shelling, grenade, and gun shots started to sound closer and closer, too close for comfort. The peace was subtly threatened. The adults listened to the radio more often. My mother and her team were warned to return much earlier. At a certain point they stopped going to the city of Umuahia all together.

My mother and my uncle had to leave in search of a safer place to live. Once again, our lives were disrupted. Anxiety and fear clouded the atmosphere. The shelling and gun shots got closer and closer. Again, it seemed to be happening in our very back yard. We stayed wide-awake most nights hoping for the best and waiting for our mother and uncle to get back. It took an agonizing seven day wait before they returned. We started to pack up our belongings. The enemy was advancing very rapidly to this town and we needed to get out as quickly as possible, move to a town further away from the war zone. There was so much panic and fear in the atmosphere that we were so glad to be moving away from it all.

Onicha Uboma

I recall that we were moved little by little to a small town called Onicha Uboma. Some of our relatives did not go with us. For reasons I did not know, there was a split. The indigenes of the town that we moved to were not very nice. Many of us had to reside in one room. At night it was unbearably hot with mosquitoes swarming everywhere. They feasted on us as flies feast on dead bodies. We did everything to try to keep them away include light up big logs of dead palm fruit hedges, hoping the smoke will keep them from coming into the house. Instead, the smoke kept us from breathing well and sleeping at all. So we slept most of the day and stayed wide awake most of the night chasing away the mosquitoes and other biting insects.

We were shown where to go and fetch water. There were two streams. One was nearby, but the water was not very clean, so we used it to wash things and to bathe, while the other was farther away. This water was clean and cool as it sprang from an underground rock. About five to six of us went there once a week to get enough drinking water to satisfy and quench the entire family's thirst for about 5 to 7 days.

On our third trip to this stream, we ran into a young man, much older than us who told us that we did not belong there and cannot get water from the stream. He looked very weird and mean. He was tall and had a bony looking face with blood shot eyes. He visibly carried a dagger and a sling shot hanging on his old leather waist belt. We asked him who he was and what right he had to stop us from getting water that runs freely. He said that he did not owe us any explanation and that we should leave. My little sister then sarcastically told him to leave. His temperament changed and he pulled his dagger and chased us for a while. We ran as fast as our legs could carry us all the way back to where we lived without any drinking water.

We told our story to the adults at home, but the next day we had to go back to the stream in the company of one of them. We got to the stream, but the terrorist was obviously not there. There was a war going on and I wondered why he did not volunteer to fight the real enemy instead of terrorizing a group of children who just needed water. Of course, that was my own opinion and the terrorist did not care, but probably got his thrill to terrorize somebody satisfied.

We lived in Onicha Uboma for a very short time, a couple of months maybe. We experienced so many difficult struggles. One day, a group of soldiers came to the door and asked for all the men who lived in the house. Unsuspectingly, my two older uncles came out. They were in their early sixties then. They were then literarily kidnapped by the Biafran soldiers, that is, they were taken against their will to be trained as soldiers only for a few days and then sent to the war frontlines to fight the Nigerian soldiers.

Our mother was not at home when they were taken. When she returned and heard the news, she ran off with my auntie to go and get them back. "We have enough young men from my family who are fighting this war" she exclaimed. They were gone for two days, but returned with my uncles safe and sound. How she did it, and what she said, I do not know, I was just happy they returned home safely. There was always a lingering fear that the

Biafran military will return for them since they now knew where they were. So, Onicha Uboma was no longer a safe place to live and my family planned another move. As was always the case, my mother left in search of another safe haven. Within a two week period we were moving again. This was the first time that we moved without the enemy getting closer to us; instead friendly fire became the threat. This town was horrible and we were so happy to be leaving it.

Umunumo Mbano

The move was hurried because they did not want the Biafran Military coming back for our older uncles. So we moved to another village called Umunumo in the small township of Mbano. This environment was very dusty. Later on we discovered that it was infested with the jigger bugs which enjoyed their residence in our feet.

The jigger bug parasite is a tiny black

flea visible to the human eye. It attaches itself on the soft flesh of the feet, preferably the toes, in between them, or close to under the nails, and then eats its way into the flesh of its host as it replaces the eaten spot with its own growing soft round white tissue in which it lays its eggs. It was a horrible tiny parasite to host.

We were told to remove them once we feel their itch on any place they attach to our foot before they grow into the flesh. We had to do a close examination of our feet regularly to catch any regular attachment. Once they imbed with the rounded white tissue, they had to be removed carefully to prevent them from busting and infesting the area of the toe or foot. They were most challenging to remove when they imbed themselves in-between the toe nail. Keeping the feet free of dust was the best prevention, but we had no shoes.

Azubike, my mother's younger brother did not heed to any of these warnings and suffered the worst jigger infestation than anyone else. It was a battle removing them from his feet and preventing new ones from getting in. He had to stay off his feet most of the time and rap them up when he had to walk around. It was difficult because we had to keep moving on our bear feet to do one thing or another, but by God's grace and healing power, we also won this battle over the jigger pests destroying our toes and feet.

The struggles in this town were producing health issues. One glorious thing that happened all through our moving around was that no one ever had the need for the hospital or a doctor's attention. We never even thought of doctors, both young and old. The jigger issue was a concern, and the constant struggle with this parasite was challenging. My family did not want to continue with it and it prompted an early move. Mother did what she does best; find a better place, hoping it would be the last.

Ife Mbaise

This time we moved to a bigger city and the compound we moved into was also bigger. The sound of shelling and gun shots was once again very far away. It was a new unfamiliar environment, but we all were relieved and hopeful. We, the children, hoped that our next move would be to go home. We had now been exiled almost two years from home.

Our arrival to this village called Ife in the city of Mbaise, was at night. We were introduced to the landlady of the house we were to live in, called Mama Ego. In the morning we met her daughter, Ego and some of her other children. We also came to appreciate our new environment because they were kind and hospitable. The house was a part of a large compound with other houses that belonged to relatives of Mama Ego. The compound setting was similar to ours back home, only bigger with better structured houses. There was also a big tree right in front of the house we settled in. There were many rooms and my mother's family settled according to how they always did, children to their own mothers in a room.

In the morning Ego and the some other children led us to some stream where we could from then on go and fetch water. In the same fashion, all of us children carried our containers to go and fetch the water. This stream was quite a distance, maybe two or more miles away.

When we got close to the stream, it was splendid to observe a huge wide open valley with a very steep sloppy path that led down to the small slow moving stream. The red earth environment was overwhelming to view from above. It was fun running down that deep wide slope with great control that could easily be lost. Coming up was tedious and most of the water spilled and wasted with the effort. By the time we made it home, we only had about three quarters to half of the container of water left.

Since we then knew the way to the stream, we were told to go on our own the next day. We got up early in the morning and headed off to the stream. We sang war songs that lifted the Biafran leader Odimegwu Ojukwu, and put down the Nigerian leader Yakubu Gowon, on our way and this made the journey shorter, easier, and merrier. As we approached the stream, there was a long line and what looked like commotion down at the bottom. This time we walked down fast and did not run. It was a hard uneasy brisk walk down that steep slope, but we made it.

We asked what the commotion was all about, and were told that the large chested man, who was in a heated argument with a group of children, both young and teenagers who came to fetch water, would not allow certain people to get any water. As we were talking with them, he saw us and left his argument with repeated shouts for them to go back. He then approached us with a slow but intimidating move and asked who we were, where we came from, and what we are doing here all at the same time, with an intolerant gesture for quick answers. We answered him very quickly, that we were refugees and told him where we stayed. We told him that we were here to get some clean drinking water for our family. He said that we have no business in this stream and that we needed to leave immediately otherwise he would harm us all. He stated that the stream belonged to him and that we should leave and go to the Imo river to get water. He then chased every one standing around to go away quickly because we were trespassing on his property and would get hurt if we continued to be there. So we hopelessly left with the other children who were also leaving.

The group that was previously sent away said they would show us the way to Imo

River, so we followed them. It was another long walk through bushes, farms, twists, and turns on a narrow bumpy path that became muddy. Finally, we made it to the river and it was disappointingly muddy water. No wonder Mr. Njoku asked us to go to Imo River; it was no competition to the water he claimed to be his. One had to swim deep into the water to get descent water that could be used for anything, and most of us could not swim, so we went home with dirty muddy water.

We told the older folks what had happened. Ego then told us to go either very early in the morning or late at night. We chose early in the mornings. For quite a while we were successful in getting nice clean drinking water without being bothered. One morning, as we were climbing up the slope, Mr. Njoku known to the indigenes as "De Njoku" was coming down. He went crazy seeing us with water and ran towards us pushing down any one he could reach. Some of us threw the water away and ran as fast as our legs could carry us. Because we were many, he was running back and forth trying to push, grab, and harass any one he could. We ran past him as he wrestled with some other children, and watched his rage go on from the top of the hill.

As time passed, a group of about twenty people came down and walked by us with confidence. As they approached, Mr. Njoku stopped his rage and then straightened himself out. They all gathered around him, talked for a while, handed him something and went on by. "Why were they allowed to go get water" we asked? We were told that they gave him money and gifts on a regular basis. That was interesting knowledge, but we did not have money. That day we again went to the Imo River, got the muddy water and went home, but with this new information.

Since there was not a drop of clean water, we had to go early for water the next day. We chose to get some of the relief supply that we had at home to give Mr. Njoku, that's if he was there. Well, he was there early on this day and giving him some of our relief supply worked. He let us through, after he counted the number in our group, and that fetched us water for a few trips. He warned when our gratuity was running out and we had to replenish. It was a tedious but temporary way of life, and again, by God's grace and mercy we survived this ordeal too.

At about our sixth month of living in Ife, we adjusted to the way things were done in this village and another way of life. My mother carried on with her routine business. She frequented the war zone markets, called "attack market" for various grains which she wholesaled to retailers in the local market places. Once she got back we would assist the adults in dividing up and transporting the various grain or seed supplies to the markets. We transported them on our heads. The retail merchants who were waiting would buy up all of the supplies. My grandmother was given a considerable amount which she retailed herself. The proceeds were used for our feeding until my mother returned with new supplies.

At evening time when all chores were done, we would sit underneath the huge tree in front of the house and sing songs of praises to the Lord from an Ancient and Modern hymn. One memorable night, it was a full moon, and as we sang, our voices pitched so high that it pieced through the night into the rooms of the compound. Many people came out to listen to us. Mama Ego also came out and clapped at the end of a nice popular song titled "All things bright and beautiful" and commended us on the beauty and vibrancy of our voices. "You all need to be in the choir" she said as she settled on a chair to listen to us sing some more. The atmosphere at that moment was also beautiful. It seemed so peaceful, ironically to say. We were experiencing so much peace in the middle of a war time. The gun shots, shelling shots, grenades, and bombing sounds were all blocked out, or suddenly seized. The night was lit up, it was unusually brighter than a normal full moon light. It was as if angles were hovering around us and lightened up the night. It was indescribably magnificent that the picture of that nighttime and moment locked into my memory to this day.

We fell asleep outside that long beautiful night. I dreamt of the war being over and we returned to a lovely peaceful home, a beautifully house furnished in luxury with many huge boxes filled with many nice things, gifts, clothes, and toys. All my dolls and some new ones with nice long hair, beautiful cloths, party or church dresses, and God said to me "it's all for you, you can have them all ". Just as I was about to start trying on the clothes, I was awakened by a soft tap on my back. "Come into the house" my mother said. I did not want that dream to end, "It had to be real not a dream" I silently muttered out. It was the most memorable night I ever had during that war time. I was very saddened to wake up just to realize it was all a dream and not real.

As we went into the room to sleep I prayed to God to please make this war to be over and to give my family and I a much better life. The walk to our sleeping place and the thought of the dream now kept me wide awake. I did not like my real world. As a matter of fact I hated my world after the world of that dream. How could I get back into the world I experienced in the dream? Maybe if I just closed my eyes, I would go back into the dream and not come back into this world, I thought, so I closed my eyes and then fell back asleep. The dream did not come back since I woke back up in the war world. There was hopelessness, living from day to day without caring what day of the week or year it was, or what time it was. There was pain, agony, and fear of the enemy whose mission was to kill and destroy us. There was the wickedness of people, those who caused this war, the soldiers without mercy who are fighting this war, the natives like De Njoku, who took advantage of the war to terrorize us and extort from us, the skinny man who chased us with a dagger with discriminating slurs to go back to where we belong, and our father who could care less whether we were alive or dead.

Why did things have to be this way? Why did we have to suffer so much? Be chased out of our homes, bombed at, shot at, and wanting all of us dead? Who would these leaders lead if we were all killed by them? Why were the leaders so cruel and greedy for gain and power as my parents had said that crude oil interests and the power to rule was the leading cause of this war? Who could answer these questions? Again, my thoughts slipped deep, into an imaginary part of the world where there was peace. I saw my family and I getting on a plane to a place where war can never be. We arrived at a beautiful mansion that had our name on the door post. It had many rooms and each room had names on it. I walked into the room with my name on it to find a beautiful cozy large bed on a fluffy carpeted floor. There were boxes of toys, a closet full of beautiful clothes, and a shelf with nice books. The house was better and bigger than the houses we lived in England. In England we shuttled between an elderly nanny, Mrs. Moore and my parents who were both in higher institutions of learning at the time. The homes were great compared to the war homes. I must have fallen asleep on the floor of the room because I woke up on a mat that was rolled out on the hard dusty floor the next morning.

I had another dream of hope in an environment of luxury. What did this all mean, would it ever come true, or was I being teased in these night and day dreams. The thoughts and the dreams were good so I chose to hold onto them both, that too was a good and hopeful feeling. It was something within that no one could take away from me. Later on in life I came across a poster that echoed from the outside what I harbored in my thoughts, so I bought it and put it up on my wall. The artist was unknown. It had a beautiful mountain like scenario with snow residue and inspiring words stating; "Happy are those who dream dreams and are willing to pay the prize to make them come true." I have been so willing and remain willing to rightfully pay that price to make my prospering dreams to come true.

CHAPTER 10

A Surprise Visitor

The following day was a nice day. My mother was home and relaxed. It was early evening when we heard some commotion at the front gate of the compound where we lived. Two military convoys were stopped at the house close to the front. A pretty young lady named Adamma, meaning beautiful first daughter, lived there. People came out to see who it was, and suddenly they started coming towards us. To our greatest surprise it was Isaac, my mother's younger brother and his body guards.

His military outfit and countenance reflected prestige and honor that commanded respect. He had driven a ferret tanker and armored vehicles, thereby attained a high ranking status in the Biafran military. He caused quite an attraction entering the compound. Adamma, had accompanied them down to show them where we lived. He talked to her for a while then she left.

It took a while for us to realize who it was. Then we screamed, "Its Isaac! It's Isaac!" The rest of the family poured out with joy and hugged him time and time again and dragged him into the house. We were all so overjoyed to see him, alive, strong, and healthy. We were so proud of him. He did not get much sleep because we had so many war questions to ask him. He told us lots of war stories too and how flying bullets missed him numerous times.

He brought us lots of goodies he claimed that they gathered as spoils from the enemy's camps, various canned foods, some kind of dried food, clothing, blankets and a lot more. We, the children, also got money, lots of money considering the high value of the Nigerian currency against that of Biafra's. He was a happy, joyful soldier and his cheerful spirit was contagious. He spent about five days with us. The first two days was with us and the last three, was mostly with Adamma who lived up the compound with her folks. It was sad to see him leave. I remember my grandmother and father pray over him, asking God to return him to his family unharmed and sane. God did honor their prayers.

Well, Isaac seemed to have taken the sunshine with him. Things settled back into the normal routine a few days after his departure and continued this way for months. One of our most interesting routines had been to go out and line up to receive various preserved food items also known as "Relief". This was distributed at the relief centers close to us or in refugee camps. We received different kinds of foods from countries that supported Biafra at the time like Gabon and Ivory Coast. UNICEF also donated a lot of relief food supplies to refugees. The most popular foods items were formulas I, II, and III made from various grades of corn meals.

The second was dried egg yolk powder. This tasted great when eaten straight up without further processing. The third most valuable was salted stalk fish and dried stalk fish.

Salt was a very scarce commodity for us back then and lack of it caused all kinds of health disorders including the infamous Kwashiorkor. A lot of salt was used to preserve the stalk fish, which made the food too salty if some of the salt is not washed out first. So we washed and saved the salty water for future cooking. The other foods we got included dried milk, oatmeal, various beans, and rice. We had to go with containers on certain days to get as much that is given to each individual or per family.

Due to the economic instability created by the uncertainty of the next day's peace there was no schools attendance. The school buildings were occupied either by refugees or relief distributors. All kinds of activities other than academic education took place in these school building structures because they were built with cement bricks. They were also better secure shelters than the mud hunt or mud coated houses. The refugees didn't have to pay any one rent to live in them.

Regular visits to relief camps exposed us to the agony the average and below average families were going through. Most of the children in these school camps walked around completely naked, economically depleted, suffered from chronic malnutrition as their health conditions also bowed to the harsh depleted environment. Some of them had balloon like stomachs with swollen feet and thin brown hair. Others looked like they had only skin on bone with thin brown hair or no hair at all. They moved around aimlessly. Most of the time, they had running noses, coughs, and running stomachs from diarrhea and other stomach issues. They were eye sore images to observe and magnetic attraction for hovering flies and sometimes vultures

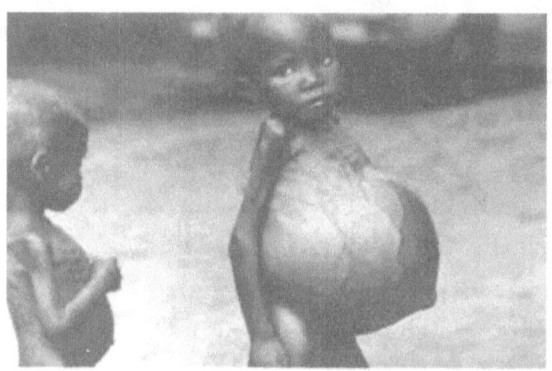

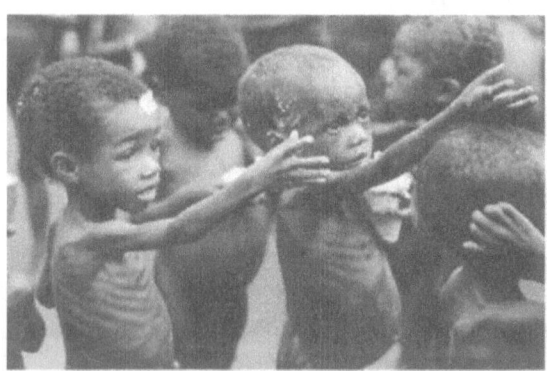

Some of them had balloon like stomachs with swollen feet and thin brown hair.

since they looked like the living dead as they walked and corpses as they laid down to sleep. Many of them did die while lying down from their ill condition. Their mothers, parents, and relatives were just as haggard, helpless, and hopeless.

God was merciful to us not to have gotten to that point of despair. He provided for us through our hard working mother whom I now know did all she could at the time. My family listened to the news and kept us out of potential territories the enemies planned to invade and conquer. After about a year of living in Ife my uncle Isaac sent my mother an urgent message to move out of Ife Mbaise because it was too close to Owerri which was going down for the second time into enemy hands according to an intercepted plan of the enemy.

Owerri

So we did. We packed up readily

waiting for instructions, Oko my cousin screamed. "Here we go again!" We were driven out of Ife to a school near Owerri Township where we stayed on transit in a camp setting with a bunch of other fleeing refugees. So far this was the worst living situation we experienced.

Our mother went out regularly; I guessed she was out looking for the best place for us to move to. Yet again, there was panic and uncertainty in the atmosphere. The dormitory style living arrangement left everything open for families to observe and stare at each other. There were so many children who were sick and hungry. They constantly cried out loud and created a noisy chaotic environment.

Outside, in the yard of the school we watched mothers cooking and some feeding their children as they squat in front of them receiving the food being placed into their mouths. In observing a particular mother feeding her naked child, she would place fufu dipped in soup twice into the child's mouth, then get the fufu, dip it in the soup and put in her mouth once. Each time she put food in her mouth the child would scream and cry. His tears and runny nose was part of his meal as he licked it all profusely when his mother would stuff the food into his mouth to feed and keep him quiet at the same time.

The food finished and the little boy had a fit. He screamed and cried, threw himself on the ground, but his mother was helpless. She needed more food herself and had no options. The little boy's crying waved in and out until he fell asleep. He shivered frequently and struggled with hiccups as he moaned with momentary cries even in his sleep. Children hardly played with each other. They stayed close to their mother or family. The countenance of people's faces were stripped of joy and happiness and replaced with visible hopelessness. I had some joy, but hopelessness was a thing that I did not have. I liked the fact that I did not have hopelessness. I guess the ongoing dreams of a better life sustained the starving hope that was in me. "The dreams have to come true" were my persuasive and fueling thoughts that kept my starving hope alive. All this was temporary. They were good thoughts because things came to pass just like I thought and dreamed.

Drifting thoughts of my future dreams were interrupted by a little commotion outside the school where some teenage children were running after lizards. Some had caught quite a few of them and some rats too. When we inquired as to what was going on, they said their mothers used them to prepare fufu soup for the family. It became the meat for the soup and wild leaves of different kinds had become the vegetables used to cook the soups. That was mind bogging because these were detestable and inedible creatures. My family did not sign on to that practice. Our mother would not even consider it. My grandparents said they would rather die of starvation. I guess we all had that option and these people didn't.

There was also a swarm of edible caterpillars on trees. A trigger shout of the village name "Wololo" would cause them to fall and there was a scrambling fight to pick them. The natives would roast them in live fire and they were eaten as a delicacy. It was determined by the local dieticians to be rich in protein. I was fascinated with the method of calling them down from the trees. I tried shouting "geeees" instead of "wololo" and it worked. I tried that because of the way they lifted their front and giggled before they fell. I was ecstatic, and shouted with joy and laughter. My shouting even brought more caterpillars tumbling down! It became apparent that the caterpillars reacted the same way to any kind of loud noise. Mothers looking to enrich their diet used them to make soups for fufu too. They said they tasted delicious. My family had options and my grandmother did not want to introduce it into our food, so the kids who wanted to, roasted and ate them against her advice. I personally did not consider them appetizing.

Well, it wasn't long before the war fire started to heat up again. It sounded like we were the closest to an invasion battle than we had ever been. Mother came back and told us to pack up and start moving on foot towards the Owerri hospital and wait in front of it if we got there before them. She had come with someone in a small car and took my younger brothers, sisters, and our grandparents. We were not to move past the hospital, but to stay in front of it and look out for this little black car and wave vibrantly if we see them first. She was so adamant about following these instructions so they can find us when they came back. It was a very difficult instruction to follow. Nigerian military invasion had made it into Owerri and were coming in the direction Mother had told us to move towards. Two of my aunts wanted to void mother's instruction and move with the crowd, but my third aunt refused, and I too refused due to the emphasis mother had put on our following through with it. We struggled through, going against the panicking crowd until we got to the spot we were asked to wait, which was right in front of the Owerri hospital.

It was getting dark. Sick and injured people were pouring out of the hospital into the chaotic crowd in the street. It seemed impossible that we could be found in the midst of all the chaos, but it happened very quickly. We saw the car moving by slowly as mother was looking for us. We all shouted towards it at the same time and that got their attention. We ran towards the car, mother jumped out and opened the trunk for us to pour all our stuff in it and get it in. As we stuffed ourselves in the car, a woman carrying her daughter with a white cast on her entire left leg rushed towards the car and begged us profusely to take her daughter with us to wherever we were going. It was one of the saddest moments of our lives and I remember it like it was yesterday. Mother was so used to helping other people and sacrificing for others, but this time I witnessed her say "I'm sorry, but we cannot take her". If there was any justification, the car was already packed up like a sardine can as we were tightly lapping each other. "Our getting out of here is uncertain, and where we were going was not safe" I heard mother mutter. The well-being of her children and huge extended family was overwhelmingly heavy on her shoulders at this time. My aunts reassured her that she did the right thing and urged her not to feel bad about it. Looking at her from the rear car seat, I didn't think that helped mother feel any better not helping them in some way.

The driver mingled his way out of the

confused chaotic crowd. At least he knew where he was going. He then drove faster as he moved past them. It seemed like an hour plus of quiet tense driving before we drove off the big road into a single lane of an unpaved bumpy road. He maneuvered around a lot of pot holes and bumped in and out of many. We seemed to be driving into a small village tucked away from civilization. It did not bother me much because my mother was in the car. I always felt secure with her around. I was confident she knew what she was doing or where we were going; whatever her plans were, no doubt, it worked out for our good and safety.

After a few miles of this rough driving, the driver slowed down and came to a stop in front of a school structure just like the one we just left. It was quiet. It also was late and dark outside. There were glowing lights on the inside. Some had fallen asleep, but my eyes were wide open. As we got out of the car the driver opened the trunk and we grabbed our belongings and followed my mother into the dormitory like setting where the rest of the family was settled. They were so glad to see us and whispered their relief with joy.

My grandmother had prepared a meal for us made of corn flour called formula II. We received the raw food supply back from the former relief camp. Our food supply was the most important thing my grandmother kept in order. Anytime we were running low on food supply, Mma Jenny let us know to make effort and replenish by finding the closest relief camp to line up and get our allotted ration. We ate up everything she cooked. When you become so hungry, anything tasted good. Everyone spoke in low voices and offered food to the driver who brought us to this temporary shelter. Since it was so late, he had to spend the night. After the good meal we settled to lie down next to them in the area they had prepared for us.

"Peace again" was my prevailing thought. Sleep was not hard to come by; it was instantaneous, deep, and rejuvenating.

Ogwa

On awakening I learned that we were now in a small village called Ogwa. As dawn snuck the sunshine in, noise was steered up with each awakening voice. Suddenly it became noisy. There were so many refugees here. We were yet in another refugee camp, a school building structure without closable doors and windows. This camp was packed with people, strange people. Some of them looked like they just became refugees for the first time, because they were healthier looking and better groomed than any of us. There was a huge woman that lay across from us. She was massive, too big to walk and laid put on a big mattress that was held off the floor with wood mounts. I wondered how she made it into this place, and I could bet she did not want to keep on running from the enemy like we had been. She had a young boy catering to her needs and he was kept very busy. As a matter of fact the whole school was busy. More people constantly moved in and settled in any open spot they could find. Fortunately no one claimed the premises to collect rent.

Everyone including my mother was there and idled time away since there was nowhere to go, no markets, no trade, no adventures, no relief food hunting, absolutely nothing to do to earn money for a living. Life just came to a standstill for everyone; still and uncertain, just like being in limbo. The tension of the limbo status was strangling our hope. Hours went by, and then days went by. News of what was going on the outside was carried and brought in by new residence. Some of it was conflicting.

Owerri was captured by the enemy the second time. We continued to hear the war music, but it was distant, ammunition, bombs, grenades, and then shelling all in rhythms. There were no more batteries to turn on the short wave radio my uncle had, so "hear say" news was our only source.

CHAPTER 11

The War Ends

Rumors that the war was over started to circulate in the camp. It was hard to believe since the rambling sounds of machine guns, grenades, and shelling was still horror music in the air. The rumor however released the tension on strangling hope. Hope in turn hung onto life with the rumor of the war ending turning out to be true.

The confirmation of this unbelievable news was re-verified over and over with many strangers who walked into the camp. Once someone walked in, people rushed to them in anticipation of better and updated news. My mother was forbidden by our family to go anywhere. For days no one bought or trusted the truth of the news as the harsh war music continued the spraying of bullet sounds, then shelling, and then a grenades or bombs. The terrifying melody of the ammunition's music kept the end of war news unbelievable. I was old enough to remember the peaceful times before the war started and knew that those sounds had to stop for the war to be ended. About a week later it did, the sounds stopped.

The tight rope around the neck of hope was at this point completely released. Signs of happiness flowed into the camp as life was rekindled with the anticipated news that confirmed that the war was truly over. My mother and sisters expressed reserved joy while my grandmother just sat on the mattress with her hand clutched to her face as if praying without showing any emotion. Mother exclaimed, "Are you hearing what we are hearing Mma?" She did not respond but started to sway her body back and forth with her hands clutched tighter to her face. She then started to sob profusely. The women knelt down next to her. My mother pulled her hand from her face and the tears gushed as they embraced. The rest of us joined to form a pack of embraced bodies weeping now with unreserved joy. As mother looked up, she saw that the men were not left out. As my grandfather was left standing motionless, his youngest son went and embraced him and the other two younger boys followed. We all stood up to complete the family pack embrace with profuse joy. This day was long expected, overdue in its coming, but the realization that it had finally come was unfathomable.

As we accepted the reality of the news, questions, many questions arose. What next? Can we now go home? If so how? Is it safe to leave the camp? What shall we expect outside the camp? Where can we get food and money for our needs? My mother usually had all the answers, but not this time. She was completely out, emotionally, physically, and mentally burnt out and out of ideas as to what to do, at least temporarily. She sat down, covered her face, and then stroked her hands through her hair confirming her loss of ideas. "Don't worry Nne Ngozi" my grandmother said stroking her back, "God will provide". Mothers and fathers were usually addressed with the name of their first child attached to their parental title. My grandmother Jenny then filled the gap and did what she could do, which was to encourage my mother with words of wisdom as she took some action. We, the children, were motivated to do the same. She took off to go and find the markets maybe to find commodities in a market place and also to get some information as to what was truly going on out there.

Mma Jenny was in her mid-60s. She was strong willed, meek, tenacious, physically fit. She was the older sister to my maternal grandmother who died at an early age with a male infant in her bosom. She married once. God blessed her with a son and a daughter. She also adopted my mother and her seven other siblings. Her husband did not appreciate her. He married a light skinned beautiful younger girl and both of them started to despise her, so she left him. She then came back to her people and served them, or rather served us, until her death. Mma Jenny was very supportive of my mother and her children.

When we got back, my mother had a surprise for us. She had gone out too and found a place for us to live away from this noisy camp. She also found out that it was not yet safe at all for us to travel back to our hometown because thugs, bandits, and soldiers who have not accepted the end of the war were operating in full force. She said we needed our privacy and safety. The place we were stationed was too remote and she wanted us to be closer to a township for easier communication and commute to real civilization, and she was right. So, a few days later we moved into an abandoned teachers' quarters, a house near a school that was in the township of Chokoneze.

Chokoneze

It was a large and nice compound with a small forest in the back yard, which had lots of towering palm trees that shaded the area creating a tropical rain forest like environment. A damply atmosphere with a moist moldy smell, caused by the humidity and the rich dark soil that supplied nutrients to the plantain trees, banana trees, palm trees, and other vegetation like vines and twigs that flourished underneath their shades.

There were also many tropical fruits growing wild. We, the children, liked to be back there eating mangos, guavas, udara a native name for a tropical tree fruit called white star apple in English. Cashew fruits, cashew nuts, and many other fruits and vegetables grew wild and freely in our newly discovered mini forest. Hunger stopped being a complaint and Mma Jenny had a variety of great vegetables to make different soup dishes. The sun made piercing efforts to shine its light through into this small dark backyard forest which became our new hangout and hideout haven.

CHAPTER 12

A Different Kind of War

It was nice to have a whole house to ourselves again. Our relatives were fewer. Many more had dropped off and gone their own different ways. I never knew why, neither did I ask. Our mother and us, her five children, my grandparents, mother's four sisters, her younger brother, and her five nieces and nephews, a total of seventeen of us moved into this teachers quarters. We were triple that number when we first left Unwana, our hometown.

We, the children, gathered around to reflect back on our almost three year journey and all the places we had sought refuge. We were able to compose a song that helped us remember the cities accordingly. We used the music of a popular song to compose the lyrics naming the cities backwards, starting from Chokoneze, where we now were. Knowing the

Song Title: From where to where
From where did you come to Chokoneze?
Chorus: Cha! Cha!! Cha!!!
It is from Ogwa that we came.
Chorus: Cha! Cha!! Cha!!!
From where did you come to Ogwa?
Chorus: Cha! Cha!! Cha!!!
It is from Owerri that we came.
Chorus: Cha! Cha!! Cha!!!
From where did you come to Owerri?
Chorus: Cha! Cha!! Cha!!!
It is from Ife Mbaise that we came.
Chorus: Cha! Cha!! Cha!!!
From where did you come from to Ife Mbaise ?
Chorus: Cha! Cha!! Cha!!!
From Umunumo Mbano that we came
Chorus: Cha! Cha!! Cha!!!
From where did you come from to Mbano?
Chorus: Cha! Cha!! Cha!!!
It is from Onicha Uboma that we came
Chorus: Cha! Cha!! Cha!!!
From where did you come to Onicha Uboma
Chorus: Cha! Cha!! Cha!!!
It is from Olokoro Umuahia that we came
Chorus: Cha! Cha!! Cha!!!
From where did you come from to Unmuahia?
Chorus: Cha! Cha!! Cha!!!
It is from Ebu-Unwana that we came.
Chorus: Cha! Cha!! Cha!!!
From where did you come to Ebu-Unwana?
Chorus: Cha! Cha!! Cha!!!
It is from Unwana Afikpo that we came
From where did you come to Afikpo
Chorus: Cha! Cha!! Cha!!!
Afikpo is our land OOOH!!!
Chorus: Cha! Cha!! Cha!!!

war was over, there was no doubt the next and last stop will be home, Unwana, home sweet home. It was a beautiful song, a song filled with hope. All the children had an input in the composition with an attempt to make it better. It got better and better as we perfected it. We sang this song day and night. The adults even joined us, some under their breath. It replaced the war songs we used to sing.

In facing reality, the war was over and God did not favor us in winning the war, but He sure favored us in surviving it without sickness, disease, or even death. Therefore, a new song was appropriate to embrace the hope of seeing home again. The hope of this belief turned to joy in our hearts and helped birthed the new song composed by the unity of happy children as we recited it together with soaring voices. We felt on top of the world for the moment and expressed gratitude in our hearts to God for everything we had.

Though we were still waiting for the

time we could go home, the end of the war assured us that this was our last stop of running from the enemy. Our waiting went from days to weeks, then months. The living conditions became rather stagnant, depressive, and even oppressive.

One late morning while we were all still at home, a military convoy with four Nigerian soldiers drove up and stopped at the front. My mother, uncle, and grandfather were told of their approach, so they came out to meet the soldiers. As we watched and overheard their heated conversation, we realized they were looking for things to confiscate and women to take with them. My mother's two sisters over heard them also and started to make quick moves to hide in the forest in the backyard. They were teenagers at the time, light skin and pretty.

One of the Nigerian soldiers stopped the argument with my mother, swiftly brushed by her forcing his way into the house where we lived. The others followed him. Their eyes scanned the house looking over the few things we had of which we had carried from place to place, mostly salvaged stuff.

His scan turned to a gaze on the mattress my mother slept on with my twin brother and sister. He ordered his men to take the mattress to their convoy. My mother started to object and plead for them not to take it since it was the only sleeping mattress for her and her children. He got very angry when she said that, then affixed his gaze on her very closely. "Because I didn't ask to take you also, you now lie that you have children!" he exclaimed in broken English with a wacky accent. Before my mother could make an attempt to defend herself, my baby brother, Stanley, came running to mother and shouting, "Mommy! Mommy! Tell Stella to give me back my plate. She took my food; tell her to give it back". Stella, his twin sister, then came right behind him promising my mother

"I have put it back for him Mommy." As her defense was made for her, their gaze shifted back and forth, from her to the now three year old twins in disbelief. "You do not look like a mother to anyone, but they validate your claim, so we will leave you alone. You may not be so lucky next time" they warned, as they finished with their interrogation. We all breathed a sigh of relief as they drove off. Well, luck had nothing to do with it because our Mma Jenny was in another room praying to the Lord and He worked it all out for our good.

From that day on, we the children, kept a vigilant day watch for their convoys. Once we saw any at a distance, we ran home to alert our mother and her sisters who in turn would run into hiding in the bushes of the small forest behind us. My grandparents were always left behind to tell them that they were home alone with the children. Sometimes they will come in and look around, and sometimes they would just drive off to their next search or conquest. Different groups came at different times.

This became our new oppressive routine. Civilians were constantly harassed, goods and belongings confiscated, and women kidnapped to be with the military men. It became a different kind of war with the same enemy, the Nigerian army, won the war and the spoils of unrestrained freedom of power over the powerless, and they grossly abused and actually terrorized us.

Since my mother and her sisters could not go out to work or find business to make some money for us to live on, we had nothing, nothing for our granny, Mma Jenny, to trade. One day, I was hanging out in the vacant neighboring school with my mother's younger brother Azubike, of whom I am the same age, and my mother's nephew, Oko, who was a couple of years younger.

As we looked up to the ceiling, we

discovered that it was made of beautifully neatly braided mats than could be used to lie or sit on. The discovery was exciting because I thought of a market place nearby where we could sell them. We successfully took on the challenge to climb into the ceiling and gently detach some, with the plan to take them to the nearby market to test their marketability.

There were so many of them, colorful, nicely braided, like new, and intact, which meant no one else had discovered them. As we got into the ceiling, detaching them without tools was hard, but after ripping a few, we found a way to maneuver the edges around the nails with insignificant damage. We got about a dozen, rolled them up, and took them straight to the market. We sold them all and brought the money back to my mother who first interrogated our story. After they were convinced that we did no harm, mother gave the money to our grandmother who then went out to buy food and other needed commodities. The school ceiling mats became our meal ticket for the rest of the days we spent in Chokoneze, the name of the small city we then resided as we anxiously waited for the green light to go back to our hometown.

The routine bored my mother to despair. She decided that she could not take it anymore, so she took the risk to go out and find a way home. She went off with one of her sisters, my aunty Mercy. I heard that they went inquiring at military bases for their brother Isaac, or cousins Sasa, Awa, or any other of our other relatives who were all military officers in the Biafran army at the time.

Their walk of faith paid off. They found where Isaac was staying, in a Nigerian military camp close by. They sent a message to him and his response was quick. He rushed to them in loving embrace, got information as to where we were staying, and then sent them home with a military convoy and a load of provisions, promising to make arrangements to get us back to our home town safely after his visit the next day. So they came home very excited, "We found Isaac" they both exclaimed with exceeding joy. "He is in a Nigerian military camp close by here, and is coming tomorrow to see where we are staying" she continued. "He is in great health, looks very well even though he is a Biafran commanding officer, he has much respect" she finished enthusiastically. We started to clean up and prepare for his visit. This was the most exciting news we had heard since the war was supposedly over. My grandparents praised and gave God the glory.

I had eaten a lot of the fruits in the backyard, formula II corn meal, and a lot of the snacks mother and my aunty brought back from Isaac. For the first time in three years I felt sick, my stomach ached and I felt very queasy. I would lie down just to get right back up again. I cried with the pain, moaned when it subsided, and waited, knowing it would start back up again. My grandmother came into the room to see me in agony. She calmed down my fears as she laid her hands on me and prayed over me. After the prayer the queasiness got worse. I felt the bowels of my intestine rise up to my throat as I jumped up and put my head out of the raggedy window located above our sleeping area and spewed all that was in my stomach. After I finished, I felt instantly relieved. As I looked at the mess behind the window I was so startled to see a big worm that had come out with the mess. It was alive and moving slowly. It was unbelievable. If anyone else had told me this story, I would have not believed them. "This is the reason we give you children Cast Oil or Mix Alba at home to de-worm you all. Since we left home, it has not been done. You should be alright now" grandmother assured me as she too seemed relieved. Though I thought some more worms like that were inside of me, I felt much better. I was alright then, I assured myself as I also received her comforting words, very alright.

CHAPTER 13

The Return Home

The next day was even more exciting. Isaac came as promised. He came with some comrades of his and with the most exciting news that we should pack up because an open flatbed truck would be here in the morning to take us home. He brought more provisions. Nice stuff we had not eaten in years, cookies that we called biscuits, candy, some yummy English chocolate, and sweets. It had been over three years since I last saw snacks like that, not to talk having them to eat. My mother made sure that everyone got a fair share of the snacks.

After the delightful treats we relaxed with Isaac listening to him tell us some more war stories. He started by letting us know that the war had ended in some places much earlier than we heard. Many people went back to their home-towns right after it was captured and some lived in hiding and never left. As the enemy moved in and out of some areas, the indigenes would move back in or cautiously come out of hiding. It was very risky and many paid with their lives for their decisions.

His life during the war was occupied with warfront fight, fight, fight. He was known as a warrior. He started like a one man army and fought like a lion, he said. When his commanding officer witnessed his bravery, he was quickly promoted to Lieutenant and given a bodyguard whom we called "back man" at the time. His bodyguard was also brave and they make quite an impact, an impressive team that continued to impress his superiors, he continued. He was put through a booth camp course on how to fight the enemy with a ferret tanker. This became his baby arsenal and he moved and maneuvered it to the detriment of any enemy in sight. He spoke in a high loud pitch voice because he had some kind of temporary hearing loss due the explosives he had to shoot out and receive in retaliation. His stories were strange and frightening. He did not seem bothered or afraid of death like we did at the time. "We fought the enemy mercilessly and fiercely. If the fight had depended on us we would have won. But we had too many saboteurs who revealed battle and war plans to the enemies. Bad, greedy, and unfaithful leaders and men" he emphasized sternly with some anger tuning up in his voice. He held himself as he wiped his face into his balding head with both hands. His frustration went away as quickly as it had come, and his old jovial self-emerged with a smile. He stood up, "We have to go back to camp and make sure the arrangements to get everyone home is falling into place." He said with a contagious excitement.

It was early afternoon so we hugged him again and again. We did not want him to leave. My grandmother held him closely and prayed over him. A tear rolled down her right cheek as she let go. She raised her hands and thanked the Almighty God for keeping him alive all through the war and bringing him back to us safely and wholesome. The gratitude to God's protection was reciprocal as everyone chorused "Amen!" in agreement.

He stepped out to meet his bodyguards who stood outside as if on watch. They moved immediately with him to the convoy. One opened the rear door behind the front passenger seat. As he got in, he shut the door and the other got into the driver's seat with his comrade next to him. Isaac turned and waved as they drove off. After we waved them goodbye, we stood outside for a while, suddenly someone shouted "let's go pack!" That jogged us into action as we ran inside. We did not have very much. Most of our goods had been abandoned as we moved from place to place. We gathered up what we had. Sleep that night was replaced by the joyous hope of seeing home again, our sweet hometown Unwana, our relatives, extended family members, our friends, our town's men and women who may have also survived the war. "By this time tomorrow" my auntie Ugo said "we will be safe home and no longer need to run into that mosquito and gnat infested forest." "Yes," agreed her older sister Nkechi, "We will be home where we belong, to a better life too." She added with hopeful relieving accordance.

The night seemed longer than other nights, but the anticipated morning came within a twinkle of an eye. The lorry came early. Isaac was not with it. Some military guys helped us load our stuff. We all climbed up into the high large open truck. There was so much joyful expectation which moved with us as the driver of the truck engaged his first gear. As he moved the truck into gear two, we did not even look back at the quarters we were leaving, there was no one there to say good bye to, no one to miss. There was a lot of space on the back of the flatbed truck, so we moved around freely as the truck moved into and around pot holes on the battered private roads. That was the least of our problems. As a matter of fact it was not a problem at all. Joy was on top of the chart and it stayed there as we bumped our jolly ride back home.

We chorused the war songs we had leaned and formulated all the way home, one song after another. If the curses and the contents of our win the war songs could kill there would not be one single Nigerian soldier or Hausa man left. The Hausas are the Nigerian indigenes that lived in the Northern region of Nigeria and predominantly Muslims. We, from the south, had very little or no respect for them at the time. We noted them as being unenlightened, illiterate, and not having regards for education. They were known to chew a teeth tainting nut called "gworo" also known in English as the kola nut. Most of them had terrible looking teeth and we used to curse them with it.

A lot of them migrated to the south with blind eyes and crooked limbs which we were made to understand are caused by the sandy and windy conditions of the atmosphere up in the north. We also discovered that many of the beggars faked their condition to gain the sympathy of the unsuspecting generous hearts that Christians have, and they were too lazy to work with their own hands, but made more money than the average working man from begging.

The Ibo man is known to have dignity and is also hard working and would not stoop that low to a begging career. They were our enemies and we cursed them in our songs and asked God for His intervention in winning the war. Well, again God did not answer our prayers that way. He kept us safe throughout the three year war period and sustained us through times of trouble and battle zones.

Even though we lost the war, we still sang win the war songs back home. We were merry when singing them; I still do not understand that till this day. Now I understand that we were covered by God's grace. His grace is always sufficient. We all must have lived off the dividends of our grandparents' unceasing prayers.

The reality of approaching home hit us as we got to the first of the two popular small bridges we call Ubeyi. We yelled with excitement and the adults who had dozed off awoke in panic, and then joined in the joyous shout. It was just a matter of minutes before we arrived into our hometown. In a little while we approached the second bridge called Itarah, we screamed again. Now we were in the boarders of our hometown, Unwana that we left a little over three years ago. Everybody stood up and gazed towards the front of the open bedded truck as we bounced towards the town. It was not like going home for

Christmas. It was very different from that. There was this mystery of anxiety and uncertainty on what to expect that kept us all quiet. As we drove into the village, it was like someone had poured iced water on burning fire. Every one of us was dumfounded. We gazed at the environment in bewilderment.

The whole place was almost leveled. An open bright environment, even the trees were gone. Heaps of red earth lay where houses used to be. There were a few houses left; some partially standing. One could just see the vast stretch of open land. It became very obvious the battle that was fought here was fierce. We wondered why this little town was so important. Was it because a former governor of eastern Nigeria, Dr. Akanu Ibiam, was from here, or was there something else they fought for? The presence of the Nigerian army was everywhere. For whatever reason it was, this small town kept the Nigerian soldiers stationed here even after the war ended. They were not only camped here, they were vigilantly patrolling everywhere. They had this base here to keep order of some sort. They moved about in military jeeps with visible double barrel guns and ammunitions hanging on their shoulders and waistline all the time.

The massive school buildings stood without the roofs and ceilings, just the shell structures. The school foundation and structure was built with cement and was able to stand the raids of the war, but the homes we lived in those days were mud homes or made with mud bricks. My grandfather's house was built with mud bricks, coated with cement, and then roofed with zinc. The soldiers had removed the zinc roofs from the houses and the schools and used them to build little box like structures we called batchers, for themselves. The persistent violent vibrations from the war ammunitions and the rains must have brought most of the houses down. This was some of the reasoning of our elders, but the rebels also tore many of them down to use the zinc to put up a shade as their temporary squatting places.

A lot of people came running to see who we were. One of them was mother's distant young cousin, named Alu. She was flabbergasted to see us and stared to scream with joy. She stopped screaming and did a jolly joy dance holding up her skirt and bending forward swaying her waist back and forth. She stopped and raised her hand up in thanksgiving and praises to God. She shouted again, danced again, and praised again. Then she went around hugging everybody and looking into the faces as she called out names as if remembering. She said she wanted to make sure she was not seeing ghosts. She would call the name again and say, "Is this you?" It was just as moving to see her alive and a survivor of the war as she was to see us.

She started to tell us things very

quickly, informing us to go to the school and get a place because everyone who had come back was squatting there. That was our only option since our home was leveled to the ground too. "People come back every day" she said, "They trickle in" she continued enthusiastically, as she listed the people whose homes were still standing and the many fears of the time. It was a lot of sad unexpected information especially of those who were known to be dead. Some of our town's men who joined the Biafran military were now insane because of shocks caused by shelling, armored car artilleries, and other war arsenals that needed to be in mental institutions. Though interesting and informative, her stories went on and on. My grandfather gently terminated the conversation by reminding them that we needed a place to settle before it got too late. So, we all got back into the truck with her and the driver was directed to the school. We found a long empty building, no ceiling or roof, no closable doors or windows. The floors were cemented and so were the walls. We off loaded the contents of our belongings from the truck into one of the buildings. The driver was urged to stay till the next morning since traveling such a long distance may not be safe for him alone at that early time of the evening, and he heeded.

The next day the men went off into a nearby farm area to cut palm leaves which were tactfully braided together into a flat mat which was used to cover the roof and shade us from the sun. Those who got back and had settled before us set this example. Our living condition was just like the dormitory setting in the refugee camps, but this time families grouped themselves together in various structures and it was a new home back at home. There was an unspoken territorial dominance that ruled the domicile of these school spaces. Once a family settled in a structure, no other family would even attempt to share the space. We the children settled at a corner spot with my mother, grandmother, and our grandfather. Mother's sisters and their children took other spots. Most of us slept on hard floors for the next few months or so. Mother still had her mattress and we enjoyed it when she was not around.

Unwana had a large elementary school with six long structures sectioned into classes representing the elementary classes of one through six. These structures have partitioned non closable windows and doorways. There was an administrative building where the principal and the teachers had sectioned into offices and spaces for work. There were also many one, two, and three bedroom homes located away from the main school structures, but within the school vicinity. These were the teacher's quarters. All these structures were built with layered walls of large 12x6x6 cement bricks and roofed with zinc sheets which were removed. These were the kind of structures the returning indigenes temporarily resided in after covering up the roof with woven palm tree leaves.

As the adults left the premises for various reasons, we eagerly arose to wonder around and satisfy our own curiosity. The first night seemed like a continued nightmare of the war in a different form, but no, it was real. We had survived and were home, a devastated home without a house to live in. Very little of our environment was livable; very few structures still existed in rugged forms except for three grave sites. Two were marble tombstones of missionaries who had died from malaria commissioning Christianity to our hometown back in the eighteen hundreds. I wondered over to the tombstone inscribed with "Rev. James White McKenzie who died at Unwana, Old Calabar 16th Dec. 1892, Aged 29 years. I know that my Redeemer liveth Job XIX 25." I thought a little bit about the 29 year old Reverend and then wondered over to the

Very little of our environment was livable;
very few structures still existed
in rugged forms except for
three grave sites.

next tomb which had "Etubom Simmers 1889." The third grave had a short iron fence around it so people did not step or sit on it carelessly. Though conspicuously located, the awareness of their existence had then interested me for an unknown reason, but I kept moving.

CHAPTER 14

Aftermath of the War

After about a week of our return, more of our relatives also returned. We found other relatives who had returned earlier than us. A routine lifestyle had patterned from our open dormitory home setting. All the adults went out during the day except our ageing grandfather. In less than a week we were told that people were now frequenting the cross river bay for various reasons, so we should take the dirty clothes there and wash them. This was our first time going there after three years of absence. We the children, always did those kind of chores; wash clothes, dishes, pots, pans, fetch water, and get burning firewood from the bushes, to mention a few. Doing them on their own was never fun for any child, neither was it for us then. The only way to make the best out of it was to have fun breaks on intervals while performing them. So we joggled all the work down to the river bay so we could swim, play, search for oysters and shrimp on intervals. We tied up the dirty clothes in a wide cloth or bed sheet and cut a sufficient piece of bar soap used to wash clothes and bathe. On our way we picked wild inedible large citrus fruits that fell freely on the ground. They worked marvelously as strong scrubs when used with beach sand in removing smoke soot off from the back of burnt pots, pans, and the taint off from iron buckets we used daily.

A broad road that was tarred with asphalt and gravels led all the way down to the cross river bay, but it was a very long route for us as pedestrians to make it to the Cross River bay. We always preferred to take a shorter cut down a steep cliff into the valley that led us to the Cross river bay through a narrow winding path road. Over the past three years nature had reclaimed this route, but pedestrians re-opened it by using machetes and sticks to initially clear the thickets and then recreate access by the foot tracking of those of us who consistently used the pathway.

Alu, our fourteen year old cousin whom we first met on arriving home, said that the environment was ghost hunted. She and her older sister, Ogwu, told us that human bones and skeletons would float around in the air, especially at night, and some would dance around in your face and then fly off. As pre-teen children, we believed these tall tales and were afraid to go anywhere, but with pressure from adults, who insisted the stories were lies, we had to carry out our chores. Due to the fear of the ghosts and bones story, we decided to go together and stay close to each other. So, we left with our buckets, basins, pots, pans, the laundry, and soap. My mother's youngest sister, Ugo, suggested that we get some long strong sticks to whip anything that got in our way. We anticipated using them on ghosts, snakes, clearing the bushes in the valley off from our pathway or any other obstruction that got in our way. The six of us; my baby sister and brother, Mary and Alex, Oko and Azubike, my little uncles, Ugo my aunt, and myself, headed down the deep steep tracks of the valley with tense anxiety and alert in anticipation of anything; ghosts, flying bones, anaconda size snakes, bush animals, to name but a few. Ugo and Mary, my younger sister, were the most fearful, and they jumped at the slightest sound of movement.

At first a bush rabbit dashed across the narrow foot path, and we panicked and screamed at the top of our lungs until the guys calmed us down. They assured us that it was just a rabbit. The poor thing was more petrified than we were. We ran backward quite a bit, abandoning the buckets and basins that we carried on our heads as we also threw away our cane arsenal. It became so obviously silly how one would have a weapon and no thought or courage to use it. With fast beating hearts and quick panting breaths, we slowly walked back with caution and belief of lingering danger. Convinced that there was none, we picked up our containers and lined back up forward down the narrow winding path. My brave little cousin, Oko, led the way. About half a mile down the road he stopped and looked into the woods on our left side. We got close to him and followed his gaze. He used his big stick to open up the bushes and revealed the dead body of a Nigerian soldier. We knew it was a Nigerian soldier because he still had his complete green uniform on with a green beret on his decayed head, similar to the uniform of the Nigerian military men that occupied our village at the time. His badges and the rank label on his shoulders indicated he was an officer of some kind, a lieutenant maybe. His body had decayed beyond recognition. It was interesting to witness what became the fate of some of those who terrorized us and devastated our town. We all stood in awe observing the details of this uniformed corpse. "This was someone's son whom they will never see any more." Ugo, the oldest of us said. "This is his grave, no one will get him and bury him properly" she added sadly. "He does not deserve to be buried" Oko quickly interrupted sternly as he poked his stick into his enlarge eye sockets as if trying to kill him again. "They tortured us and devastated our town and now they are occupying our land and harassing us. All of them should end like this one" he continued, as he poked deeper into his skull without fear. I was terrified of it, and so were the other girls. Oko poked harder and his head fell away from the body. We screamed in horror, and ran away as if there could also be a resurrecting moment. The brave guy also stopped; a bit frightened of the movement he activated himself. Azubike pulled Oko away from this messy activity and urged all of us to progress on our chore. "He is already dead and there may be many of them in this valley" he concluded. I wondered how many other people died miserably in this valley, both military and civilians. This was added confirmation that our town was a heavy battleground, one that changed the lives of the indigenes forever. I began to strongly believe the stories of ghosts and flying bones at night. The thought of encountering them was haunting and mindfully disturbing.

As we approached the river, we noticed that the bay which used to be farm land was covered with thickets, giant shrubs, and tall wild grass that had grown undisturbed for the past three years. There were a few cleared areas where bay farmers had already sown new crops in the ground. The river kept the bay surrounding well-watered. The farms down at the river bay produced bountiful harvests because the grounds were kept very fertile as dead fish and river animals' remains washed up and decayed on the land. As the harmattan season approached, the water receded exposing the middle sandy island and a very fertile river bay where farmers planted crops they were able to harvest within a six to eight month period.

Since the middle sandy island was not yet visible we stayed at the river bank and did all our washing. We loved to play around and swim until our eyes became irritated and uncomfortably red. After about an hour or so of swimming and playing we became hungry, so we packed up to head home. With basins of cleaned wet clothes and buckets full of river water on our heads, we headed up the steep hill. It was always more tedious walking up steep hills with heavy loads on our heads than coming down. As we got to the dead soldier's domain, we all steered into it, my guess was to make sure he had not resurrected. Our thoughts must have been the same as my aunt confirmed aloud, "He's still there." We hurried past him. Hunger and weakness increased with every step, but we persevered and made it to the top. Some of us were almost out of breath and energy. We put down our containers and rested at the top of the cliff.

On looking down into the valley we just came from; the trees, shrubs, and thickets now looked small and were no longer threatening. Even the narrow winding road we had just walked was barely visible. There was a relieving feeling and replenishment of power and control from the top looking down and being distant from what we all knew was a death infested environment. I imagined all the dead bodies in the valley, their hovering ghosts, the snakes, and the wild animals that had grown massive by feasting on them and their carcasses. It still was a haunting thought and I did not want to carry on with it, so I impulsively shook my whole body in an attempt to get rid of the heavy thoughts and the weight it heaped on my tender mind. The compelling and grateful thoughts of being a war survivor must have deposited some supernatural strength into my weakening and hungry body because, instantly, I found the energy to keep moving. The others might have felt the same. My sigh and movement seemed to jog the others out of their hypnotized state, because some also sighed and followed my move to go home.

Adding to the weight of these thoughts, we put our containers on our heads and headed home. As was in the past, prior to the war, many greeted us all the way till we got to our new domain at the school compound. Tradition was not lost, nor was it gone with the war. That was a comforting observation well pondered in my heart.

The Bell and the mine fields

Mma Jenny was not the type of person who sat around and did nothing. She was urging to visit some of her farms to see what the grounds and the seedlings looked like. My family pleaded with her not to hurry out or go to the bushes or anywhere else yet. She took their advice and stayed back for a few days. She also claimed she felt a warning in her spirit not to go farming just yet. It was a great thing she did not go because bad stories started to unravel.

After about two weeks or so of our return, the death bell rang early in the morning. Our hometown had a big bell stationed on the cross road of the main narrow tarred road and private dusty road leading to the administration building of the elementary school. The bell was rung to signal the occurrences of different events. If there was a call for an emergency town hall meeting, for example, the bell would be rung fast one time after the other continuously without any intervals or pauses. People and the elders of the village will then pour out to the town hall to get information as to why the meeting was called. If someone died, the bell ringer would pull the ringer cord twice with a waiting interval of about two minutes pause then ring it again twice. He would stay with this pattern of ringing for about fifteen to thirty minutes. By the time he finished, the identity of who passed away would be revealed to the inquiring minds. If the person was well known or related to someone who was well known, you would then hear screams of agonizing cries and wailing from a distance from various directions.

The bell was rung during the early morning hours this time. It was the first time in three years since we last heard it. Many of the people living close and around the bell, and also those who heard it ring from afar came running to find out who it was that died. The ringer stayed on it for a long time.

His companion quickly started to narrate the sad horrifying death of his younger brother. They wanted to go to their farm to survey the condition of the land and crops. As they walked, they tried to create a path with the large sticks as they came upon a covered up path. They then cleared the thicket out of the way and proceeded. As his younger brother following him, they heard a "click" sound followed secondly by sudden explosion. On turning around his brother was lying in a pool of blood with both his legs chopped off from his knees. They were alone, but the explosion had caused a few others in a distance to come running. He knelt down helplessly over his brother who was screaming out in pain. He loaded him up in his arms as he was panicky and screamed encouraging words for him to hold onto life and not die. Other people in the woods arrived on the scene. The huge unraveled ground from the explosion of the booby trap landmine was an unquestionable answer as to what happened. One helped him to carry his bleeding brother whose loud screams had then turned to low moans. Another person held onto the amputated bleeding legs as they all hurried back into town for medical help. By the time they made it out of the farms, the victim's moaning had stopped, the gushing blood from his legs were just dripping. The raw open ends of his legs were mixed with dirt and clotting blood. He became non responsive to the encouraging words to hold on. As they moved with him, his body became heavier and lifeless. By the time they got into town his spirit had left him.

They moved on to take his body to their domain. They left a trail of blood and mourners as they made it to their home, with inquiring minds that followed them and helped spread the sad news. Indigenes then realized the woods were laid with land mine traps. He told his story crying and wailing at the same time. The elders asked the bell ringer to ring an emergency bell since everyone needed to be informed. People gathered at the base of the bell. The Nigerian military, being suspicious came around too with their guns corked and ready to shoot. But quickly and bravely the elderly chiefs who were there made it known to the indigenes the caution they needed to heed on going into the woods. The gatherings and meetings were stopped; also was the ringing of the bell, as long as the Nigerian military occupied our village, because they would not allow it or the unity of our meetings. They were uncomfortable and threatened by the meetings.

My grandmother was blessed not to have gone into the woods to survey her farmland. She was always a blessing to us and we loved her dearly. She was the greatest helper to my mother. My grandmother knew how to depend on the Lord while my mother knew how to depend on her. I chose later on in life, to learn from my grandmother on how to depend on God. She taught me many things; how to braid hair in the reverse corn row style, how to serve other people and her family without grumbling or complaining, she exemplified how to be meek, how to love unconditionally, how to do hard and smart work with your hands, how to give with a cheerful heart no matter how little the contribution.

I also learned many wise native proverbs from her. She used to say,

"An okra stalk can never get bigger than its master because, even as it grows taller, the master can always bend it down to pluck the okra off of it".

When people acted crazy around her, she would firmly keep her stance in word and deed stating that,

"A mad man, woman, or a drunkard still has his or her senses." In other words, he or she knew what they were doing and would not cross a fiery boundary.

When she sent us on errands, we had to pay close attention to the message and get it right the first time, if not, she would send us back with the expression, "A child who does not know how to execute their errand properly will have to make multiple trips".

The adults did not let up in sending a child back on the same errand until it was done right; neither would they take it from them to go do it themselves. The child had to learn the hard way by going back over and over until it was done right. Repeating a task over and over was like punishment and very tiresome. Sometimes we brought multiple complaints to her about different wrongs a particular person had done to us. Mma Jenny would then repeat the Igbo proverb that translates,

"When an ant stings the butt, it then becomes mindful where it sits." The lesson was that you do not keep going back for more stings after the first or second bad one: Just learn to stay away from the stinger. There were many more Igbo proverbs Mma Jenny used to caution us, advise us, and encourage us in concurrence with Proverbs of the Holy Scriptures. She was an inspirational model of how a woman can be beautiful on the inside with a glowing reflection on the outside as she exemplified the Christ like sacrifices needed to selflessly care for our large family and others. In now understanding God's virtuous woman, she measured up as one of them. Her character was perfect, her integrity polished to a glossy glorious shine no one can miss, her words always uplifted and built up the hearers. I can simply say that the glory of God radiated His countenance through her. We thanked God for preserving her life from the farmlands that were turned into mine fields. She later lived to be ninety three and I am honored to pay a tribute to a woman of God, our wise grandma Jenny.

The mines continued to go off in different places at different times. It was the most devastating aftermath phenomena of all the rest. Men, women, young adults continued to be casualties of the mines laid in the pathways to the farms. The irony of the whole

A Tribute to a Woman of God
Our Wise Grandma Jenny

situation was that these victims survived three years of civil war and returned safely home just to die painful deaths or be handicapped from residual war arsenals spitefully buried in the pathways to our farmlands.

CHAPTER 15

Back To the Farms

Our grandmother much later on returned to the farms, but was never a casualty to the landmines. God was always good to her and protected her going and coming. We all believed that. She invited me several times to go with her. The three years of war had brought about a change of desires into my heart. I no longer wanted to do such things. I now wanted to go to the city and attend school. We had lost time, school time, fun time, peace time, and so on. I guess, my priorities were changing as I was growing up. Sometimes I reluctantly went with her anyway. The cassava farms we went to had cassava still in the ground. The harvests from the farms were very dry with little moisture and almost a waste to prepare them for gari or fufu, since they were over three years old. She said the tubers were over mature. The harvested crop was manageable to eat, but not profitable in the market. Mma Jenny did what she could and promised a better and faster harvest since the grounds were now much more fertile, and her prediction with the harvest turned out to be true. The yams farms were even worse than the cassava farms. The yam tubers rotted in the ground. Had they been out of the ground and aging in a barn they would not have rotted. Therefore, most of the yams were rotten and re-growing wild. The vine of the yam must grow winding on a tall vertical stick to produce good large tubers. The ones growing were crawling on the ground and the yams were small in size and unprofitable for the market and consumption.

The Palm Tree

There were many red palm tree plantation farms that belonged to the local government's department of agriculture. The trees in these farms did not grow tall like the wild tall towering palm trees we see in fancy pictures, post cards, and all over the Southern Nigerian Region. These short palm trees produced very healthy heads of palm fruits at or below eye level. It was rumored that there was some sort of germ manipulation of the palm tree used by agricultural scientist to breed the fruitful short palm tree. It was forbidden to pluck them for any reason, even to snack on them. This was the government's way of protecting their investment. Only government authorities were allowed on the palm tree plantations. Individuals caught trespassing were arrested and prosecuted as thieves, but after three years of war, the plantations were not harvested, so the fruits blossomed and then rotted. There was also no management or law enforcement. The palm fruits became food for all and free for all. No one came forward to apprehend violators. Though most of the crops were over mature, the indigenes made the best of them to get all the products and byproducts from the palm tree. It was a very interesting and lucrative crop to learn the processing to its profits.

The palm fruits are imbedded in-between a large head cluster with sharp thorn pricks sticking out above the fruits as if protecting them from predators. As the fruits become ripe, their color changes from a dark brown to orange, and to red; and they become easier to pluck them off the clustered head. The fruits are then put in a large wood mortar and systematically mashed with a large pestle so that the red skin and pulp are released from the hard shell protecting the kernel nut that nature placed in the middle and not breaking its shell. Water is added to work up the separated pulp which is then sifted through a perforated calabash to separate the pulp from the chaff. The pulp is kept in the sun to stand for a while as the fine rich palm oil rises to the top. It is then separated from the pulp and stored, while the pulp is a rich paste like sauce

These short palm trees produced very
healthy heads of palm fruits
at or below eye level.

also used to prepare various soups for fufu and other meals.

The quality and taste of the palm oil depends on the condition of the palm fruit itself. It cannot be prematurely or over maturely harvested. Premature palms fruits produce very little oil. Over mature ones start to rot at the base of the fruit and the rotten taste finds its way into the oil and pulp.

One of the purchase tactics of palm oil Mma Jenny taught me was to steer the oil to determine how much pulp it has, and then taste it for freshness by dipping your finger in it. A deceptive selling scheme would be to put the palm oil in a large basin and leave it under the sun for the pulp to melt and look appealing to the unsuspecting buyers. The quality of a soup or meals prepared with palm oil depends on the quality of the oil purchased at the market place.

The palm fruit can also be enjoyed raw as a snack. The palm kernel is sheltered in the middle of the fruit by a very hard shell which can only be cracked by smashing it in between two hard stones or other hard objects. The mature nut is also hard, but enjoyed by many who like to exercise their mandibles. It takes lot of chewing to break down and swallow the little nut.

When palm kernels are roasted on an open pan, dark oil is pressed and released from it, which the indigenes believe to be medicinal. The dark oil is stored in small bottles and given to anyone who is sick to drink from spoons and rub on their bodies supposedly to ward off germs and help in recovery. The palm kernel oil is also sold at the markets in various size bottles for various prices. The hard broken shells from the kernel are only used to keep cooking fire alive; though it burns slowly, it maintains a glow.

The Palm Tree branches when pilled together and woven into braids are used for roofing hut houses, mats to sit and sleep on, and other things. The trunk of the long or short trees do not burn but smoke profusely, thus cannot be used for fire wood, neither does the spiky empty head of the palm fruit have much good use. As the life of the trees comes to an end, they are cut down and the stumps can make great farm seats, tables, and short bridge logs to crossover small farm streams.

A lot of the tall palm trees grow wild. It takes a skilled climber, who ties a strong heavy rope around his waist and the trees with a comfortable gap in between. He would move the rope up the tree as he alternately takes steps up leaning backwards on the rope. He makes consistent upward moves in this manner until he gets to the top then checks the status of the fruit or taps the wine from different kinds of palm tree that has palm wine.

There were more wild trees than skilled men who were willing to climb them at the time, so was the multitude of ripe fruit not harvested. So, the fruits would fall to the ground and be carried away by chipmunks, squirrels, and other animals that also desire them. The kernels were found all over the place, some would find fertile grounds and grow back up wild into fruitful trees. If the land the trees grew on belonged to someone, the trees ultimately belonged to them too, otherwise it was free for all.

Another war aftermath dilemma

My grandmother did not do the palm oil processing very much. I observed her once process palm oil when she bought some of the palm fruits from those returning from a palm fruit harvest. As we were coming back from the market, my young cousin, Oko, came running to help get the bag of palm fruits she was carrying on her head off as he greeted and comforted her with relieving words at the same time. "Jokwa ooh! Mma" he said repeatedly, meaning well done mom. He had been out and about and heard a lot of new disturbing stories about the occupied Nigerian soldiers. They were rough soldiers, better classified as rebels, who had no conscience. They moved with the wind as they made their own oppressive demands from the civilians. New recruits, their superiors, and the ones in-between all acted obnoxiously towards us, the indigenes. This time, they were forcefully taking and raping our women and young girls. They forcefully took them for their sexual pleasures and relief. The elders of the land were very angry and called an emergency meeting about the pressing issue. They sent delegates to talk to them. "It is forbidden in our land for sexual union of any kind without marriage" they were told. That was our custom prior to the war. If any unmarried girl or woman was found pregnant she was brought before a panel of elders and questioned for the father of her child who was then summoned to the same panel. Their parents were then made to unite them in marriage whether they wanted to or not, but the case here was different, a crime against the all the people. The Major who was the commanding officer of the battalion station in our hometown was consulted and told about the violations of the young girls, women and traditions of the land. He laughingly promised to talk to his military men, we were told. Their language changed but the crime did not stop. A Nigerian military man would see a girl he wanted to be with, forcefully take her stating, "I will marry you for two days, or one week, or two weeks," but this was continuous rape that degraded the young women of our hometown to victims of sexual depravity and then abandoned with emotional, physiological, and mental scares for life.

The crimes produced an outcry. Our women were kept out of their sights. The Christians cried out to God in our ravaged Presbyterian Church building. Some of the strong men took matters into their own hands to find terrorizing tactics to scare the so called hooligan Hausers away from their immoral sexual violence. Some villages went to their idols and witch doctors for solutions to this horrible matter. I do not recall how long this lasted, but one day, the army battalion packed up and left.

A great fearing man of God, Dr. Akanu Ibiam, who was once the Governor of the Southeastern Region, was from our hometown and was still alive and had returned home. Due to his polished integrity, his influence and power was much more impactful then than it was when he was in office. The height of his integrity had no match then neither is there any today except maybe the ordained Presbyterian Church Priests and Ministers of God. We believe God's intervention must have worked through him for the removal of these military criminals and our kinsmen and women were grateful.

Marriage and Tradition

Even as a Christian, a recognized marriage in our town is a big traditional deal and couples to be must go through four phases. The first phase is when the groom to be goes with his friends with bottles of wine or some other drink to introduce himself to the bride's parents and make his intention known and then ask for their daughter's hand in marriage. Information is exchanged at this point. Parent's names and background information is given and received for background checks to be done on both sides. The background check includes but not limited to; character investigation, religious belief, sickness and disease genetic, generic or inherited curses, and other family ties.

If the background checks are satisfactory to both parties, the groom proceeds to set a date to provide the bride's dowry according to the guidelines given by the bride's parents. Bride pricing is set according to the personal value parents place on their daughters. Some put steep bride prices if their daughter has been highly educated or extremely beautiful. Some may be reasonable bride prices no matter how highly they value their daughter, but demand an acceptance, care and love from the entire groom's family.

The third stage is the wine carrying. This is a joyous occasion where the bride and grooms family and friends come to witness whom she has chosen as her husband. It is the heart of traditional marriage sponsored mostly by the bridegroom and his family. There is a long menu of activities on the program and long speeches of affirmation and approval from both sides. It is not just the unity of two people, but the unity of two families getting to know each other because they must also look out for each other's welfare from then on.

As the ceremony progresses, palm wine is put in a cup and given to the bride to go and search for her suitor sitting in the midst of his peers and identify him by giving him the cup of wine she is carrying to drink. With loud and elaborate music, she dances her way towards the young men and teases some as if giving them the cup, but withdraws before he, being the wrong person, can grab the cup. There is laughter and cheers as she dances to the direction her fiancée is sitting. She dances profusely in front of him upon locating him then hands him the cup of wine. As she lets go of the cup into his hand, there is great cheer and joy as he drinks up the wine and joins her in the dance. The guests also join the dance with money in their hands with which they spray the bride and groom as they continue to earn the dance money. From then on the ceremony is dance, dance, and more dance! Merry and joy dominates the occasion until the night is danced away.

The fourth and final stage is when the groom then gets to receive his bride. This stage is called "leading the bride home". The bride's parents over time accumulate various items including different kinds of fabrics and clothing that a new bride will need to run and live in her new home. Her peers also contribute gift items and are also the ones who carry all the goods bought for her and then lead her to her husband's house. She is then recognized as married once they arrive at her husband's home.

Some of these stages can be combined or done all in one day if planned properly. Christians top the traditional marriage by also having a white wedding in a church setting in God's presence for His blessings. If a Christian skips the traditional wedding, the elders, peers, and indigenes will not recognize the bride or groom as married and will consistently bother the families for their share of the bride's wine and gifts. It is not a position parents of the bride especially want to be in because future intervention and problem solving of marital issues between the bride and groom are usually settled effectively when the right people are invited to counsel them, elders and their peers and others who witnessed them get married.

This is why our elders became very upset the way the Nigerian military men were treating and disrespecting the daughters of our land. This caused the outcry that got rid of them. Average people in our hometown are decent, respectful, and mindful of their social conduct.

Child bearing

One day a pregnant woman who was newly married to a young man across the street from my great grandfather's compound went into labor. My grandmother Jenny knew them very well and had witnessed their traditional marriage. She was having her baby in the enclosed backyard of the house they lived in. Many women, friends and relatives including my grandmother went to sit around and welcome the new baby. Their home was packed with women who took turns in encouraging her to labor on. The women who showed up wore a white powder like substance called "Nzu" around their eyes. Any one seen with this makeup was usually asked who is having a baby. Mma Jenny took me along, but did not ask me to put on the nzu. When the labor pain intensified we would hear the mother to be screaming for relief and help. "Sorry," I heard a woman say "this is a pain you must bear all by yourself. No one can help you even if they wanted to takeover for a while, but stay encouraged we are all here with you and for you," she said.

We heard the conversations, but only the experts in delivery, her mother, and mother-in-law were allowed back there. They were careful in holding her hand because her grip during labor pains could dislocate the helper phalanges or wrist. Just before delivery, her screaming intensified as the compassionate experienced mothers empathized and shouted out their persevering encouragements. As the baby was pushed out and cried, the women in the room got first hand news of the baby's sex. "It's a boy!" they shouted from the backyard. With that information the women collectively shouted the announcing song called "Okokoriko" as they formed a circle and danced, flagging white handkerchiefs as they swayed their waists back and forth. They came prepared with musical instruments and took the birth announcement outside the house into and around the whole neighborhood. It was a joyous occasion for both families who graciously welcomed their new member.

The mother of the new mother usually stayed with her daughter and her new grandchild for up to six months to alleviate her other burdens and then help her ease into motherhood. The same is done even when consecutive children are born to the same person. Women, till this day, understand the pre and post-natal trauma that can befall women of child bearing age, and they unite to intervene and prevent any of that from occurring.

CHAPTER 16

The Rebuilding Of Unwana

Many of us lived in the open school structures for months. There were no doors or windows. The top or roof was covered up with braided palm tree branches to shade us from the harsh sun. The braided palm branches were not overlaid in the manner to prevent the penetration of rain. Everything gradually became routine and the environment somewhat conducive. Some of the teacher's quarters remained unoccupied because people said they were isolated in wooded areas and haunted. We the children, stopped being afraid of the environment and started wondering around at our leisure times to pick fruits and vegetables that grew wild in the bushes.

One day, we chose to explore the isolated surroundings, so we wondered into the so called haunted teachers' quarters. We went from one building to another as if looking for something. They were open cement structures of small two or three bedroom homes. There was nothing in them; no toilets, fixtures, nor ceilings inside. The windows were without panes and sheets. The insides were clean, probably washed clean by the rains. As we went into the last house on the end of the quarters, we stumbled unto what we were looking for. There it was, a complete human skeleton. It lay straight making a triangle at the corner of the room. It looked like he died lying straight on his back. The white bones were as clean as the floors of the structure. All the bones lay there complete and intact, from the skull to the phalanges.

"His relative would never even find this one to bury either," I thought. All his flesh and clothing was gone; I'd rather say rotten and washed away.

"Why did animals not devour his body and why did these bones not get up and fly around as our relatives had lied to us?" I asked. I then stared at it intensely to see maybe that I had spoken too soon as the bones may still get up and come after us. It seemed like my question triggered all of us to think the same way and expect the same. Our gazes caused an unusual stiffness in the air followed by quietness that temporarily sealed us into a hypnotized state. "There you are!" he shouted suddenly. That was a frightening startle that jogged us out of it with a terrifying scare. Azubike, my young uncle, who said he did not want to go along, had changed his mind and came looking for us. He was frantically running from one structure to another because he knew we were somewhere out here and did not want to be alone. As he rushed into our discovery, he screamed with joy in finding us as we in turn screamed with fear. We grabbed him and ran out of the deteriorated building at the same time, telling him about the skeleton which also seemed to have moved with all the commotion. He said he too wanted to see it, so we summoned up the courage and went back. We were definitely carried away by our imagination because it hadn't moved. "It looks like a man, a very tall man of over six feet," he said. After about ten more minutes of analyzing him further our interest shifted to getting out of there, so we hurriedly went back to our safer domain.

The rainy season was almost over without any rain. My mother had left to go to the city to start trade and promised that once she found a place to live, she would come back and get me to start school. I was very excited about that, and desperately anticipated it actually happening. The youngsters of my age had missed three years of school. As she left this time, I was not worried, I was hopeful.

Two days or so after she left, in the middle of the night we were awakened by a very loud noise. We got up in fear. Suddenly there came this bright light that flashed across the sky. Its reflection pierced through the braided palm branches that partially shaded the roof. The flashing light was followed by the same loud noise that awakened us. It was thunder and lighting, strong and vibrant. Almost instantly it began to rain. Heavy rain, big drops of gushing rain poured for about two long hours.

The roof we had was not made for rain it was made for the sun. We all stood up inside the school structure, soaked with the pounding rain as it made its way through the roof which could not hold an ounce of it. It was warm water and that made it bearable. We all stayed standing till daybreak. Everything and everywhere was soaked. The same had happened to everyone around us. No one was ready for rain or even thought of it.

Late morning the sun shine came out very nicely. The atmosphere was cleaned, the dust washed away. God had given us a wakeup call, reminding us that nature was still His making and that we should make ready for all inevitable seasons. We laid all our belongings out in the sun. Before evening, most of the place was dried by the intense sun and the extremely dry weather. The sleeping mats were dried and the clothes, even the big heavy mattress seemed dried.

Men from different families headed to the woods and farms that morning and brought back more braided palm branches. They dismantled the batchers Nigerian military soldiers built with the zinc they yanked off the roofs of our houses and schools and used the old rusted zinc to make better roofs. Many started to build homes in their individual allotted family compounds. You could hear the clattering of knives, the pounding of hammers echoing from different locations.

As I had always observed, the indigenes from my hometown could never be classified as lazy people. In a very short period of time new structures of houses of different shapes and sizes sprang up everywhere. The vast land that lay bare as we drove into our hometown then had a different look. There was no town planning required, no zoning ordinances to observe, no city permits to wait and pay for. All that was needed were willing hearts and hardworking hands.

Most villagers rebuilt their homes made with mud bricks and roofs with braided palm tree branches or other heavy grass plants. Their only cost was the labor of their own sweat, and they labored diligently and perspired profusely. Many vacated the schools within a couple of weeks and God held back the next rainfall till most of the hard workers put up their rain proof homes.

CHAPTER 17

My Last Days living in Unwana

Over the years, Unwana indigenes constructed great modern homes with contemporary fixtures and fine finishing. These cost money and professional labor to build. Many people also left our hometown and moved to bigger cities to work for wages or attend higher institutions of learning in order to further their education. At the time, Unwana only had an elementary school.

My mother had found a place to live in a city called Enugu. She also started trading on various fabrics this time. She had promised that the next time she came home I was going to leave with her to start school, and I was ecstatic about that news. I could then envision my war dreams coming true. One day we saw a car drive up to the school area where we lived. There was a driver and someone next to him pointing toward us. The car drove up close and in the back seat was my father. He came out of the car and walked towards us. I stood there looking at him. I was not sure what to think or say. I could not run to hug him, nor did I feel cheerful in seeing him. It was the first time I had laid my eyes on him for over three years. I found the voice to say, "Hello papa." He smiled and approached me slowly. He asked if this is where we were living. "Yes," I replied. He then asked for my mother who was in inside. I shouted out loud for her and she came out. My uncles, grandfather, and grandmother were all out on chores. I heard him talk to my mother for a while. I did not like what I was over hearing, and my temperament changed for the worse. My small mind started to strategize very quickly. My mother then called her three oldest children which included me, and said we should get ready because our father had come to take us back with him. I looked at her, pleading for rescue with my eyes.

"What about my war dreams that just seemed within an arm's reach, had he come to shatter them?" I asked myself in my thoughts. He was not in my dreams, nor was he in my plans, as my thoughts continued to race before me.

Mary and Alex, my younger sister and brother went away slowly and sadly to do what they were told. As my mother continued to talk to him, I moved very quickly to the side of the school building which hid me a little bit. The rest of the land was open, but I did not care. I started to run slowly. As I looked back, no one had noticed that I had left, so I ran faster and faster until I got to a house where I knew I was out of sight since I could not see the school any more. I knew they could not see me either. I stopped running but my heart did not, it pounded and raced before me. I headed straight to Ude's family hut house, a distant relative that lived deep in a small village called Ezi-Ukwu.

I had built great relationships with many villagers and they were always glad to see me and feed me with their special native foods and delicacies. Their mothers, grandmothers, and great grandmother were always great hosts to be around. Ude was the name of a young girl who served my mother as a maid before the civil war started. Our fathers were somehow related because they had the same last name with us. Her mother was always joyful to see me. Most of my family members did not come into the remote villages, but I did, and I knew my way around. I did not tell them why I was there, I never needed to. Ude was home and was about to go to a nearby small open market called 'Ahia Epe' to run an errand for her mother, so we went together. It was not towards the school, it was in the opposite direction. Her mother wanted some ingredients to make Egusi soup for a fufu meal. As we got into the little market the women and young girls would pull on us to patronize their products. Ude's mother had also taught her how to be a pro buyer in order not to be conned by dishonest traders. She approached the young girl with some unpeeled melon seeds we call egusi. After inspecting the seed she asked for a full cup of a small measure of an empty evaporated milk can. She poured it into a paper, skillfully made into a cone style wrap, then bent the ends to secure her packaging and gave it to Ude in exchange for some money. The trader opened her waistline, took out her cloth money belt, and added the money to the rest of the money she already had in the belt, and tied it up securely before putting it back in her waist. Ude purchased some gari, crayfish, some dried fish, a small bottle of palm oil, some green vegetables tied up with its own vine-like stem called ugu, and then we went back to their hut. She helped her mother prepare the ingredients used for the soup. She took the egusi seeds one by one and systematically peeled off the light brown skin covering the inner beige edible seed. When she finished, she placed them on a big flat smooth stone, then used a smaller roundish smooth stone to blend the melon seeds into a paste. She worked this very fast with both hand and pressure from her arms. By the time she was finished, oil was oozing out from the egusi paste. She processed the onions, pepper, and crayfish the same way, then put them all on different sides of the same dish. She then cleaned out the dried fish and removed most of the bones, and then put it in water with the blended onions, pepper and some salt.

I was helping Ude separate the vegetable leaves from the stem or vine. As we completed that, Ude washed the Ugu in a small basin, and then put it on a long piece of wood that was placed across the emptied clean basin. Then she started to cut the ugu into the basin. She would take the cut up vegetable from the basin and chop it up some more. The cooking fish started to smell very good. She opened the pot and added some palm oil then the blended crayfish and let it simmer some more, then she opened the simmering pot again and added the blended egusi which turned the color of the soup. It was like adding milk to the red boiling soup. The egusi thickened the soup somewhat, and then she put in the chopped vegetable which was the last ingredient. After about five minutes of adding the vegetables she replaced the pot of soup with a pot of water. The soup smelt really good, and I was hungry. When the water boiled, she poured gari into it, shook the pot and drained out the excess water with some chaff that sailed to the top. The gari hardened into rough dough like fufu.

Food was ready and we enjoyed every bit of it. Everyone ate out of the same clay plates that were placed in the middle. We took the gari from one plate and dipped it in the soup that was placed in another plate.

During the meal they asked if I wanted to go again with them to the fishing expedition at the muddy Lake Okosa since the season was almost near. As we had returned home, they both took me to the most adventurous and memorable fishing trips I had ever been. Before the rainy season comes and goes, the water volume in this muddy lake rises and recedes leaving enormous amount of various fishes in it. So, twice a year hundreds of indigenes travel on foot miles away to Okosa Lake, located on the outskirts of Unwana, with small but sturdy strong fishing scoop nets and containers. As we got into the mud bare feet, the fish would hit our legs as they swam around. The muddy water level was at waistline, sometimes higher but always manageable to walk in. At first it was very scary. Ude's mother showed me how to keep my scoop net down in the mud until a fish or two wiggled into it and then swift up the net quickly. It was very challenging to keep them in the net. The fish were strong, agile, and sometimes too heavy for my young hands to keep them. Due to the rush in the lake, they swam around frantically like they knew it was survival of the fittest for them... but I was ecstatic to catch some. As we were going home with a load of fish, I told them that I'd like to go again, but now things had changed, so I rescinded the offer.

At the end of the meal, the older person usually shares the meat or fish, but Ude's mother took some fish and left the rest for us to share. This was how most families traditionally ate, everyone from one plate be it with hands or with cutleries. If a family was eating and a visitor walked in, he or she was always invited to join the meal; no matter how small the food portion was...unless they declined to join the feast. If they joined, more fufu would be made and soup poured in the bowl to satisfy all who were seated to eat.

I was physically, emotionally, and

mentally exhausted, so I laid down on their hard mud bed that was covered with a woven raffia mat and fell asleep. They let me sleep. I am not sure how long I slept, but I heard Ude's mother telling her to wake me up and escort me home because it was getting late and my people would be looking for me, so she did. I was rested, but still too anxious to go home, I reluctantly and slowly got up. As I stretched and pumped up my body, I wondered what the next hours had for me. As we got close to the school, Ude hugged me and said goodbye, then we parted, and I hurried back to my domain.

My father's car was gone. I was not sure if it was just gone from this location and around someplace else. I was expecting serious scolding and disciplinary action to be fiercely taken out against me. When I walked in, to my greatest surprise, my brother Alex and sister Mary were still there. My grandmother and uncles were back. Everyone was home except me. They all looked up and I could tell that things were not quite right. "Where have you been," my mother asked sharply. My uncle interrupted with a smile and a confusing comment that I was not expecting. "Wherever you went to, you saved the day."

Everybody at the same time started to tell me the story of what happened, but my uncle brought that under control by hushing everyone to be quiet. Then they took turns with him letting me know that my disappearance caused a delay that allowed time for their return and intervention.

"It was wrong for your father to go his own way all these years and leave his family, then come back for only three of his five children and not his wife" he said in a loud angry voice. "No" he exclaimed. "He has to abide by our tradition" he continued, "He has to come with wine, goats, and all of the things on the list we will give him, apologize to this family and make promises or vows to take care of all of you otherwise he gets nothing," my uncle finished.

My grandmother took her turn of telling how he ignored their order and chose to take off with Mary and Alex who had already packed, but they stopped him and said no. Alex my brother jumped into the conversation to tell me how he dragged his hand and my mother rushed for his other hand and they were pulling him back and forth until my uncle came out with a big stick to hit him, then my father let go of Alex, walked quickly to his car and left in rage and shame. My uncle Richie had asked him who was going to care for us, and he said he had someone who would. Apparently he was living with yet another woman. The thought of a living scenario without my own mother was not negotiable. I was so glad to have dammed the consequences and did what I had to do; consider it childish or civil disobedience. It was quite a dramatic day and the selfish thoughts and action of my father was absurd.

I already had the vision of seeing myself in a new city and a new school and no one was going to take that dream from me. So, I held on to it very tightly, in thoughts, words, and in action.

About a month or so, my father snuck into town and kidnapped my younger brother Alex, in broad day light and in front of many witnesses. My uncle Richie sent an urgent letter to my mother who was now spending a lot of time in the township where she was seeking business opportunities. The urgent letter was sent via a self-employed driver, named "I Shall Return". We abbreviated his name "I Shall" He shuttled passengers daily to and from Enugu, the city where my mother was then residing. The post offices were not yet functioning efficiently at the time, so he also serviced our communication needs. Alex's kidnapping was very bothersome to my mother's family who believed they had failed her in the care of her children.

We lived in a society and a time where the intervention of law enforcement was not even a consideration for solving or resolving such civil matters. Family intervention was always one sided. It was tit for tat and survival of the fittest. The family with tough family alliance and domineering influence prevailed over such tyranny. Alex, my brother, was about nine years old at the time and all my mother and her family did was make unsuccessful attempts to kidnap him back, so he temporarily lived as a servant boy in the control of the woman my father then called his wife. Alex later told the horrible stories, how she treated him like a house boy, a bus boy, and a boy to market the petty goods she had to sell to make extra change since our father didn't give her enough money. Our father never paid attention to family matters and what was going on with us when we lived together with him, and he never did later. So Alex lived at that woman's mercy and our father's non-mercy.

Later on in the years that followed, my father expressed that he held me accountable for his failure to get his children back at the time he wanted. He wrote me a long letter in response to a long letter I had first written him. After our high school literature study of 'Things Fall Apart' authored by Chinua Achebe, the character of Unoka, the irresponsible and lazy father of Okonkwo, a brave Warrior was comparable in my mind to my own father. I was angry at him and despised the shame he brought on our family and his people with the selfish and ignorant choices he made. I presented to my father a ten point similarity of him being like Unoka. He typed a long response letter back to me in black and red ink on legal paper sheets years after I wrote to him. He tried to defend and rebut all the points he could, but the ones he couldn't, he would thank me for abusing him with it. At this time, my mother had great progressive plans for me that corresponded with the dreams and prayers that I had for myself. My mind had already grasped the hope of a great better future life as I had been dreaming and I was not going to allow anyone get in the way of that. So, I really cared less about him and wasted no energy thinking about his feelings which was mostly egotistical anyway. To him, life revolved around him. I was so fortunate to be put out of his vicious revolving orbit; to be sucked into it again would be grave.

The conversion

A few months after our move from the school building into a newly constructed hut on the lot of our great grandfather's compound, we were spending some leisure time wondering around the vacant, ravaged school structure as we noticed some vehicles parked at one of the buildings. Some groomed looking people had arrived and were moving back and forth carrying stuff from their cars into a small quarter of the school. As we observed from a distance, they worked like ants; diligently, with unity, and focus. They moved in chairs, tables, boxes of stuff. The commotion and loud music was intentionally attractive. The movers looked up and with an inviting smile motioned us to come.

There was a big banner stretched out across the wall with "Riches of Christ" written on it. An evangelist named Edozie had set up his ministry. He had quite a few helpers who offered us seats to sit and wait. Their set up was very impressive and many curious people came strolling in as their inquiring minds also wanted to know, like we did, what was going on. In less than an hour all the laid out chairs were taken. There were many who did not mind standing and with time, the standing audience grew larger than the seated one. As the arrangement was set, Edozie stood up in front of the people with large sheets of roll over white papers in his left hand and introduced himself as Pastor and Evangelist Edozie. He also introduced his cheerful helpers, whose names I do not remember, one after the other. He continued by telling us about his God given mission to tell people about the true riches of Jesus Christ. He lifted up the giant booklet in his hand as two of his helpers moved swiftly forward, took it from him, and then held it up with one person on each side. He turned the first white blank cover page over revealing an enlarged handsome half image of the European art version of Jesus with blue eyes and long blonde hair. He then started by introducing us to Jesus. How the Word of God, was sent into the world to dwell among us in flesh in the person of Jesus Christ. He explained to us that God created us in his image, as a spirit being, and a living soul with a body. Our spirit being cannot die and that our soul includes our will power to make our own choices. That makes us different from other animals that do not have souls and will power but only instinct. God's purpose was to have a loving Father and Child relationship with man, of which he first had with Adam and Eve, the first man and woman he created, he continued. God blessed them with a fruitful paradise garden called Eden to dominate, feast, and enjoy the fruits from any tree except one known as the tree of good and evil, he preached on. These instructions were given to Adam before Eve was birthed out of Adam. God promised that the day they ate of it they would surely die. They listened to the lying serpent, who was the Devil, instead of God. This brought God's curses on them and all generations of mankind to this day.

"We are all born into this world inheriting Adam and Eve's curse of eternal death, death of the soul which is the real man," Pastor Edozie assured us with a sad tone in his voice. Then he looked around at the quiet and intense gazing audience. He picked up a bible from the table set beside him and turned the pages to John 3:16 and shouted out loud,

"But God so loved the word that he gave his only begotten son, Jesus Christ" he added.

As he called Jesus Christ, his helpers lifted up the huge booklet, with Jesus' image, up as high as they could.

"That whosoever believeth in him shall not perish, but have everlasting life" concluding the scripture. Joy eased into the hearts and loosened the tense audience as they cheered with praise and applause. That continued for quite a while. Pastor Edozie let the crowd enjoy the good news for a while, and then continued in a louder voice that caused the audience to further listen as his helper turned to another page of the huge booklet revealing a man with a bad spirit and its filthy belongings in his heart. He said that was how a man is without Jesus, but when we hear the word of God and receive it, the bad spirit will go away because the word of God is truth and bad spirits cannot dwell together with truth, so the truth drives him away and sets the man free from the bad spirit.

Pastor Edozie's helper turned the booklet to the next page that revealed a man with a heart nicely cleaned out. He then continued to tell us how the spirit that went away wondered around restless and was tormented in dry places because he could not find another human heart to house himself, so he came back and found his formal house nice and cleaned out, but he was afraid of going back into it by himself. So, he went and found seven other spirits more wicked than him and they went in and that man's heart was hardened more than it was before to the word and work of God. Again, the audience was attentively tense and quiet with super glue gazes to the beautiful graphics of the vivid images of eight bad spirits in the heart of a man on the new page that was just turned over. It was an image that invoked a ghoulish feeling of loathe. As he looked back into our drooped faces with a long pause in his speech, Pastor Edozie broke the tension with a smile as his helper turned the page to a man with the same image of Jesus now in his heart instead of the eight demons and said,

"If you receive Jesus Christ into your cleaned out heart and these evil spirits come back, they cannot come in because Jesus will not let them. Isn't that great news?" he asked with intensity. "Yes oh!" we all shouted in agreement with another long cheers, praises, and another round of applause. He then asked for all who wanted to receive Jesus into their hearts and make him their Lord and Savior to come to the right side of the building. No one stayed behind. Even those who came in late and did not get the full message came forward and gave their lives to Christ. It was a glorious day for me and so many others. My life changed for the best on that day. Due to it being a period in time when dates were of no concern, I do not remember the date, but I recall every detailed moment of my becoming a true Christian by my own choice because I heard the gospel presentation that day. It has stayed imbedded in me because it was my new spirit's birthday. I did not just believe in Jesus Christ, I now know that I am redeemed by his precious blood and that my Redeemer lives. It then became clear to me why I lingered around on the tombstone of the late twenty nine year old Reverend James White McKenzie who died at Unwana delivering the gospel in 1892. The scripture inscribed on his tomb "I know that my Redeemer liveth" was now inscribed on my heart. I then understood the connection, it all came together; from Job who professed this in Job 19:25 to Rev. McKenzie in 1892, to me in 1970, all drawn to the same Spirit. Nothing could assure me more with this confirmation that my soul was now safe and secured under the blood of our Lord and

Savior, Jesus Christ. To be completely forgiven of Adam's inherited sin, our personal present and future sins, I then embraced the true Riches of Christ our Savior with my whole heart.

My Departure to the City

Becoming a born again Christian was an instant change for me. I repented completely. The conviction of The Holy Spirit was very strong, and God always has a firm grip of my hand. In the later part of my teenage years into adolescence, I let go of God's hand and did my own thing, but He never let go of mine. Before then, I wanted to be in God's will and always wanted do the right thing though it was sometimes difficult. As a born again Christian a lot changed, my friends who could not talk me out of it went away since I could not convince them to become what I had become. The places I desired to hang out changed, the recklessness of my speech, and my way of living changed.

Born again Christians were labeled and isolated as members of Scripture Union abbreviated as SU. I guess the SU name was birthed from the persistent study, teaching, and referencing of the Holy Scriptures also known as the Holy Bible. Though I never denied the term, however I preferred to be called a follower of Jesus Christ also known as a Christian, a true Christian, born again Christian, or Consecrated Christian. Edozie and his followers left. I had no one to personally teach me the scriptures. I guess no one knew how much I wanted to learn, understand, and emulated what I witnessed him do. The desire to witness consistently burned in me, a desire that God fulfilled in the mid part of my life with what I nicknamed 'midlife Christis' as Jesus Christ's ambassador and witness. Mother noticed the change in my behavior when she came from the city. I had no convictions for standing up my earthly father though I much later forgave him for how he treated my mother and abandoned us, his family. I also prayed that I could get his forgiveness for any wrong I did to him. My act of civil disobedience paid off big time though. Mother now had a place to live and had found me a school and I was to leave with her in a week's time. In addition to the good news of attaining salvation, this was thrilling. My joy was full and my dreams were now coming true. Hopelessness completely lifted and evaporated like smoke disappears into the spans of the atmosphere.

I spent the rest of the week going from one home after another bidding my village and town friends and relatives goodbye. They were sad to know that I would not be visiting them for a long time because they enjoyed my visits and vice versa. I promised to come visit them any time I visited home. Yes, Home! Unwana is home, home sweet home, where people loved one another, looked out for one another, gave to one another, and covered one another. I did encounter a few detestable people with ugly and twisted minds, but the majority of indigenes that I was drawn to who also embraced me with love were overwhelmingly plenty. Even the civil war could not and did not ravage those relationships of great accords. The sweet memories and cherished thoughts of the people I got to know would keep a dose of warmth in my heart and a wealth of unseen grin on my face. If I were to practice thinking about them, I had more than sufficient pleasant thoughts and people to meditate on a daily basis for a lifetime.

As I left home with my loving mother at the end of that week to continue life in the city, I slid down into my purchased seat in the 404 station wagon Peugeot of "I Shall Return" with Enugu as its destination. Before the vehicle moved, my thoughts shifted its own gear and moved into a cross road of sorts. Though I would miss the people, the excitement of what lay ahead was without a doubt, beds of roses in greener pastures, as the life in my dreams actually begins," I thought. My adopted attitude was that I had a spot light shining on me and when it periodically went out the halo over my head would become visible. I had confidence without knowing it, an inviting temperament without feeling it, and a hopeful future that I always knew did not depend on me alone. As life's bed of roses presented its thorns of harsh lessons, my future hope stayed anchored in the right place. I choose to remember the good, happy, and merry times; and then leave the bad, ugly, and cynical with those it belonged to. The wonderful memories of my "would be" ongoing encounters of life would add with those of our sweet home, to compile a colossus memorabilia over time.

"By God's sufficient grace, I too shall return to my home sweet home, whenever and to whatever it will become, since life will move on as I have chosen to move on," I thought. I Shall Return had finished loading his vehicle. As the passenger loading servicers banged on his hood to move his car, they jerked me out of my long deep thoughts. I became alert as he ignited his car, engaged his gear, and we zoomed off. The war was gone, Unwana life behind me, and the unknown, "here I come!"

Chapter 18

That Was Then and This Is Now

I was eleven years young when the Nigerian and Biafran war started. Now, I am seasoned with years of great experiences, vast knowledge, unique understanding, godly wisdom, and the blessings of life's trials and tribulations. God has also blessed me with four loving children. I have learned lessons both easy ways and in very hard ways. I have learned to be liquid in my expectations of humans, what life under the sun brings, and to hold onto material wealth with appreciation but loosely.

I have been blessed abundantly above and beyond the desires I dreamt during the civil war. Upon finishing high school at Anglican Girls Grammar School in Enugu, our principal bid us farewell at our final assembly gathering with a heightened awareness that we had been sheltered within the fenced premises of the boarding school, and at the time, being released into the world. We did not really understand what that meant. To us it was an exhilarating release to freedom of which, we seniors, frequently high fived each other exclaiming the word "into!" on a regular basis.

Boarding school was like a suffocating cage. Many of us joined various school societies that frequently took us on events outside of the cage; like the Debating Society which gave us the opportunities to visit other schools and mingle with other scholars, while the Geographical Society took us on excursion to interesting places like factories, industries, and breweries to see how things were made or manufactured, and the Girl's Guide which had regular meetings with students from other schools to learn how to be ready helpers to the society we lived in and to each other. Those of us who were members of these societies had regular fun with the extracurricular activities which made us believe life outside the strict boarding house was a bed of roses. So we were ecstatic with the thought of permanently leaving it to go into the world to later experience the pricking thorns of the rose beds.

A few of my close friends left the country to further their education in the United States of America. My continued communication with them shifted my dream into the next gear and my dream wheel turned to the USA as I learned about the American dream and adopted it too. I have been privileged to come to the USA and achieve the American dream to a point, realizing most of them; houses, cars, money, and stuff, just to turn around and lose them all. The losses, fiery trials, and long tribulations brought me to my right senses.

I had let go of God's hand as life in the world was deceivingly good and rosy. I became prodigal to Him and sought to find

Him again as thorns of the marriage rose-bed pricked deep into my soul. It took me a while to realize that God never let go of me. He was still holding onto my hand. On listening to Reverend Fredrick K. C. Price's and Dr. Charles Stanley's ministry messages, I rededicated my life to God and toned up my spiritual faith muscles which has enabled me to hold back on to God's hand tightly, never to let go again.

One day I asked my youngest child, who was fifteen at the time, to tell me anything he could remember of his youngest age as a child, toddler, or infant. I was amazed when he responded saying, "I remember being carried on your back." From the time my children were a week old till a little over two years of age, tying them on my back, with a two and half yard wrapping cloth, was always a convenient way for me to protect them from getting into any kind of mischief. It was also an easy way of putting them to sleep, and a

I was amazed when he responded saying
"I remember being carried on your back."

convenient way of caring for them while I got a lot of domestic chores done. Whenever I wanted them to sleep, I would carry them with their hands tucked in, otherwise I left their hands out for their convenience. They enjoyed the position of being clung to the warmth of my back, and watched me as I worked.

Back in the days during the war, I observed pregnant women carrying their toddlers on their backs and a ton of load on their heads, and stuff in the hands, walking to and from the markets, farms, and to fetch water for their families to use at home. Some made very long distant trips in this manner. At this point, I thought how privileged I have been to live in America, a place where the taps provide clean drinking water on demand, electricity is powered on and off as needed, and visible dust does not hang in the air. The dream of a better life has come true. Compared to what I had then, I now live above and beyond my war dreams, the American dream. Although living in America has its own constraints and challenges that can breed its own hardships, I still prefer to live in America even with the challenges, as I gain the advantages of striving for the big and ultimate dreams of enduring wealth as I have now learned it to be.

However, what I had learned from my son's response is that a child's memory can go so far back into early infancy. Children soak up every minute detail of life occurrences like a sponge soaks up liquid and then drips with the excess. As I pondered deep into my own memory bank, I was ecstatic as to how rich my childhood storage section contained. It was loaded with the good, the bad, and everything in between.

Children remember faces, beautiful faces with cruel hearts and hurting hands, ugly faces which first scares them but calms with soothing voices that reassure that there are people with loving hearts. Children remember voices; threatening, harsh, soft, soothing, angry, and loving. Children remember stories; tall tales, real, and personal stories. As a child we believed them all at first, and then sort them out later in life. Children may be afraid to say, but they remember good and bad conversations or communications. Children are the most vulnerable of any segment of society; they are always trusting, the most fearful, naturally shy, physically weak, utterly dependent, and so very easy to please.

All I could do as an eleven year old child was listen to the anxious conversations of my parents, our neighbors, my teachers, and others, then react and live with the terror of war threats, of promised death, and ongoing daily devastation. Now, as a matured adult who has survived a war, I take on this blessed opportunity and a cause to stop any war from ever brewing in the mind of any man or woman who is privileged to read this book.

With empathetic understanding, experiences, a witness to the devastations, tragedies, and consequences of war, I qualify to protest the declaration of any war that is not initiated from the stance of a genuine defense.

Nothing is ever won by force. War is force, it is destructive and pollutes. It creates nothing but problems. It holds back, pulls back, and knocks down what has been built up. It harms and hurts everyone and everything, the hunters, the hunted, and anyone that gets in the way since innocent civilians are mostly used as shields and vengeful targets when the leader and military forces who are supposed to be the main target become elusive.

I do not believe there is ever a winner of war. One soldier's death on one side is someone who could have lived for a noble purpose if they had been directed or redirected into a righteous path in their early life. Upon our return to our devastated land, the marble tombstone rock on the hill remained intact and cried out the name of Reverend James White McKenzie, who brought the message of life, will be forever remembered for his contributions as a love messenger. In contrast the soldier, who brought war and devastation to our township, ended up dead, unknown, and unburied in the valley of Ugwu Ebe.

The negative lingering aftermath of wars breeds deep hatred between the invader and the invaded. The tangible and intangible spoils cannot compensate enough for the intangible consequences afflicted by subtle aggression that indefinitely continues from the oppressed and resentful losers. The minds of many fighters, both soldiers and rebels, become futile. The wounded, both physically and mentally handicapped later become a burden to their families and the societies they return to. What spoils, benefits, or rewards can they enjoy?

Since the Nigerian and Biafran civil war, modern technology and acceleration of information has taken the sophistication of war to the highest level of destruction to man, the environment and our earth. Whether it will be chemical, biological, or nuclear warfare, any of these may now have the capability of wiping out an entire nation, a continent, or even lay the earth bare. Even the so called cold war had its own destructive power.

What are we fighting for?

Motives can be hidden. A man whose thought is consumed with the quest of destroying another and the environment of others is a cause of war that is by itself wicked and selfish; this type of wickedness originates from minds that have inclining self-destructive ambition. These are tyrants who cannot live and let live. The smell of death is their thrill and the environment of destruction is their green pasture.

Coveting the spoils of another's treasures is another leading cause to many wars. Having the ability to oppress and legally or illegally confiscate the natural resources and belongings of others increases the zeal for war just like the taste of blood ignites the zeal to kill for more blood in young carnivores.

Territorial dominance and enlargement have also been ongoing causes of wars. Simple examples can be selected from little toddler bullies in a kindergarten classroom, gang rivalry on the streets, and kings of kingdoms with the inclining desires to enlarge their territories by taking over the territories of others. Since greed does not satisfy, a conqueror's scope of territorial rule may keep increasing until his or her domineering thought turns to an obsession to rule the whole world and attain absolute power.

Many aggressors underestimate the resisting ability of their potential targets and find themselves struggling to complete their mission, or even to save their own lives as the presumed weak defendant puts up a life and death struggle. Some may be defensive, but they relentlessly struggle, aggressively or passively, thus we see wars that linger on from months to years to decades. This type of ongoing struggle causes both sides to become weary and oppressed. The indigenes of the war territories, their neighbors, and their environments also become oppressed, hardened, and numb. Children caught in war environments or born into them are deprived of normal lives styles with common necessities like clean water, fresh air, decent meals, basic security, mental and physical health.

I witnessed what the war did to the people that I knew, loved, and looked up to as adults. Some of the young men from our home town never returned. Their grieving parents and relatives could not get used to the void their loss created in their homes and lives even till this day. These parents should also be considered as emotional and psychological war casualties. War initiators can never project the extent of casualties and the devastation of their decisions. The negative effects are deep, wide, and rippling. Our family had the loss of Nnanna, who was to marry my aunt. The only picture left of him is the one our minds held onto. If there was ever a black and white photograph of him, it was destroyed along with everything else we had. I'm not sure whether to consider us fortunate comparing to the loss of others. Some families lost all their young men. Though we did not lose ours to death, we lost many to insanity and different kinds of mental health alterations.

We frequently went to the psychiatric hospitals to visit some of our relatives who were committed into the mental institution after fighting in the war frontlines due to their deranged minds which included, delusion, amnesia, hallucinations, depression, physical violence, and other mental disorders. To this day, though they are now middle aged men, they still seem to be missing part of their brain or mind set and this shows up in their behavior every now and then.

If the minds of young adults can be so traumatized by war artilleries and arsenals, what of the mind of a child who lived in terror with the constant threatening war music of bombs, artillery, shelling, and grenades going off one after the other in successive days and nights for years? Personally I had frequent tormenting nightmares of air raids and running from the enemy after long the war and into my adult years. I constantly had dreams of the fighter airplane zooming into my airspace, spraying its bullets or dropping bombs on us. I would sometimes be unable to flee and the fierce attempt or struggle to find cover would manifest in real life as I would abruptly wake up and thank God that it was just another nightmare and not real. With a pounding heart, I would try to go back to sleep dreading the re-occurrence of these air raid nightmares. They only started to fade and then completely stopped as I sought the grace and mercy of God through consistent and fervent prayers. Peace and wholesomeness of mind, body, and spirit has now completely encompassed me. What could have been my fate with a mind of constant trauma that these nightmares had brought into my soul? Thinking about it now, I could also have been a patient of the mental institution as an unrecognized casualty of war, and a lifetime patron of prescription medication for mood swings, mental disorder, or schizophrenia.

Under similar circumstances many children, who survived wars, have grown up without any kind of psychotherapy and currently live unfulfilled lives; blaming war makers, their parents, or even society for causing them to suffer through the trauma of a war they did not originate nor have anything

Who are we fighting for?

to do with. This is what war survivors, who live in or out of war ravaged environment do, blame someone; and truly, someone is accountable. They grow up in a war cycle and then relay the war cycle to future generations. These cycles need to be broken by resisting the startup of wars from within.

Who are we fighting for?

A picture is like a thousand words. Some Biafran war pictures portray Briafran soldiers with their guns walking by children dying from starvation, disease, and other war consequences. As a child I witnessed and survived the Nigerian and Biafran civil war. I grew up to hear about the devastations of World War I and World War II. Hitler's quest for absolute power devastated his people, his victims, and himself. The spoil from the Vietnam War is a bitter gall with its residue that lingers on in the mouths of our veterans and the people of Vietnam till this very day.

More gall is spewed up from the lingering Afghanistan and Iraqi wars. The recent raging Syrian war has depicted images of thousands of helpless fleeing refugees drowning and the beautiful body of a three year old child that washed up on the shore making headline news. Wars in the Middle East have birthed many battles that have raged on and off and yet they are still fighting. Thousands of lives of children have been lost, and some of those alive have been emotionally traumatized permanently for life.

I once got a call from a veteran who fought at Desert Storm in Iraq. He wanted to see a house listed by Century 21 Judge Fite, a real estate company I was licensed with at the time. He expressed that he had VA pre-qualification housing benefit and was looking for a home to purchase. I met him and his wife at the property they called for after a short phone interview. He was a young tall man, seemed to be in his early thirties. He was also handsome with detailed muscles and an intimidating body size that portrayed perfect fitness. I unlocked the door and invited them in. It was a beautiful newly constructed custom home with large rooms. As we got to the master bathroom, his wife motioned him to the shower. He said the size looked good, because the shower comportment was large, above average size. She urged him to go into it and shut the glass door, and he did. Within seconds he swiftly zoomed out, and then moved all the way out of the house back into the parking lot. She followed him, and I followed her. At first I was shocked to see him sobbing with a petrified temperament until I remembered he was a veteran. That shower enclosure had steered up emotional or psychological trauma the Iraqi war had dumped on him, just like our relatives from the Biafran war of over forty years ago. How can this veteran enjoy any house or his life? It does not matter which war it is, the negative lingering effects are the same. From the Mongol Conquests to the modern wars of this day, man still has not learned that nothing is won by force. Preparation is now being made by different nations of the world to destroy other nations in a massive destructive way. If this is ever allowed, chances are, the earth will be laid bare by atomic fire.

Those who have wars within them as a norm must wisely be introduced to the reality of an existing peace. Political debates puts out the call "Hawk War" for war or "Dove War" for peace. If given the opportunity to revise this political metaphoric terminology it would be "Hawk War" for war and "Dove Peace" for peace. Apparently the mind that birthed the slogan has a war norm mindset that introduces the word "war" even when introducing or initiating peace. "Dove War" is the same type of peace the world system introduces to us. Peace while anticipating war, peace with anxiety, the type of peace that tells you the war is over but you still hear the shelling, grenades and ammunition music from automatic rifles in the quietness of the night or ongoing nightmares that forbids sweet sleep. It is a false peace that can never satisfy.

There is another peace, a peace that surpasses understanding, the peace of God. This is "Dove Peace" given to anyone who can receive it. All who are introduced to it and receive it can replace the war norm with it, and then become truly liberated. It is one of the greatest blessings an individual or nation can have. Individuals can sleep through storms with it including families who have strived in unity with fruitful legacies. CEOs are productive and profit with this peace, and kings rule wisely when they seek and find this peace and as they implements it, their kingdom flourishes.

We can only get what we give. We can also only find if we seek, and doors will open if we knock. If we knock on doors with peace treaties, we shall establish covenants of peace. At any level of life, if we implement the "Dove Peace" we can establish a stance where even our enemies can be at peace with us. Who are we fighting for? There are loud voices advocating for the unborn in churches and congressional platforms all over the world, meanwhile the children caught and born in war zones are dying in silence, both physically and emotionally. Massive numbers are dying as orphans from starvation, pollution, insanity, sickness, disease; and lack of knowledge of their existence. Some pictures of the deprived children slip through the cracks to tell their stories and lend a voice to their 'silenced' cry. Children are our future generations. Their mind, body and spirit needs to be protected from any kind of war damage. Let the strategic fight be against war that kills their bodies, deranges their minds, and devour their souls. Let us lift up our voices and advocate for this segment of our future generation, children in war ravaged environments, by speaking against war of any kind. Again, nothing is won by force, but love for one another can win anyone over, including an enemy. People do not care how much we know, but will always want to know how much we care.

Knowing that the seeds of war would much later produce bountiful harvests of toxic fruits, is it not wise to avoid wars at all cost? I am urging the readers to have a changed mind on starting an offensive war of any kind but to advocate and help save the children already caught up in war environments and prevent new casualties. If our readers can in one way or another stop or prevent a potential war, within one's self, within a nation, or the long waited world war III, this book will achieve its purpose.

About The Author

Elizabeth Abamu, considers herself blessed to be a survivor of a brutal civil war. Their father, Lloyd, was granted a private scholarship to further his education abroad, either in the United States of America or England. He chose England because of the fierce ongoing apartheid in the USA at the time. He took his wife and daughter, one year old Elizabeth, with him. She was privileged to spend the next nine years of her life in England. Her father graduated with three degrees in Law, Librarianship, and Journalism. Her mother studied domestic science, after which they returned to Nigerian. Two years after their return, the Nigerian and Biafran civil war broke out and lasted three long years. Elizabeth is grateful to God for not only being a survivor of this brutal war, but also for preserving her memory with every detail of her childhood experiences and observations of the Nigerian and Biafran civil war. Elizabeth expresses how bad experiences of human wickedness inflicted in times of war can ravage the mind of a child and leave residual nightmares and other mental disorders that can linger on into adulthood. God brought good out of her bad experiences through the love and legacy of her godly grandmother, Mma Jenny, and her loving mother. As a team they made up the hedge and stood in the gap as both mother and father to their family. These war experiences have blessed Elizabeth with the ability to empathize with other children and to continue praying for their sanity as they strive through and survive the torments and traumas they do not in any way help create.

Elizabeth, a graduate of The University of The District of Columbia in Washington DC, is also a Minister of God, His word, and His works with a life purpose to serve with

Christ Jesus and bring about a positive change for the people who cross her path, particularly children in war ravaged environments pocketed in various parts of Africa, the Middle East, and other parts of the world where wars and poverty have hit hard. This is part of her passion of ministry. With a loud voice we collectively plead to all, for the sake of the children, to "Stop the Wars," all over the world and "Save the Children."

References & Picture Sources

It would be hard to establish the original sources of some images because they are linked to multiple internet sources and various media outlets.

Front Cover picture: icrc.org
Bomb: hangthebankers.com
Yam Farm: hopefornigeriaonline.com
Yam Barn: Flickr.com/International Institute of Tropical Agriculture.
Heap of Cassava: active.constantcontact.com
Dr. Akanu Ibiam: flickr.com/creativecommons.
Fleeing Refugees: umcmission.org
Starving children with hands out: doynews.com
Starving children from malnutrition with stomach disorder: meniru.blogspot.com
Palm Tree with fruits: biofuelmerchants.com
Woman carrying child on her back: flickr.com/creativecommon
Soldier passing by dying children: slow-journalism.com
Hungry and dying children: igbofocus.co.uk

WAR FROM A CHILD'S POINT OF VIEW

AMERICAN JOURNAL *of*
TRANSFORMATIONAL LEADERSHIP

PRINTED IN THE UNITED STATES OF AMERICA